TRADERS
THE JOBS
THE PRODUCTS
THE MARKETS

David M. Weiss

New York Institute of Finance

Library of Congress Cataloging-in-Publication Data

Weiss, David M. 1938–
    Traders : the jobs, the products, the markets / David M. Weiss.
    p. cm.
    ISBN 0-13-926320-9
    1. Stockbrokers—Vocational guidance—United States.
    2. Stockbrokers—United States. I. Title.
    HG4928.5.W45 1990
    332.64′023′73—dc20   90-34287
                                                                  CIP

This publication is designed to provide accurate and authoritative information in regard to the subject matter covered. It is sold with the understanding that the publisher is not engaged in rendering legal, accounting, or other professional service. If legal advice or other expert assistance is required, the services of a competent professional person should be sought.

From a Declaration of Principles
Jointly Adopted by
a Committee of the American Bar Association
and a Committee of Publishers and Associations

Printed in the United States of America

10 9 8 7 6 5 4 3 2 1

New York Institute of Finance
2 Broadway
New York, New York 10004-2207
A Division of Simon & Schuster, Inc.
A Paramount Communications Company

To those who take
the time to explain . . .

Contents

Preface

Traders is an introductory source for anyone who wants to become a trader. It will introduce you to the trader's role and to the multifaceted trading process. The book explains in plain-English the various investment products that are offered throughout the securities industry. This information can help you select a field, such as options, in which to specialize. And, unlike most other books on the subject, Traders describes the trading environment in true-to-life ways.

This book will dispel some myths about trading and show that those myths can be replaced with a firm understanding of the reality of the trading world. While much of the trading process is based on judgment, that judgment is based on an understanding of facts, data, information, and so on. Only after the trader has digested all this information can a sound judgment be made.

Trading also requires a discipline that takes into account human frailty. A good trader must be mentally sharp in his decisions but not emotional. An emotional trader will most likely let irrelevant data enter into the decision-making process thereby clouding the true picture. Many traders, however, display great outbursts of emotion when some expected result happens or doesn't happen. What is important is that emotion is a result of, and not a part of, the decision-making process.

While traders do not have to be great math students, they must possess an understanding of the relationships figures and prices have to each other. By applying this aptitude to the product being traded, the trader will be able to predict the probability of an event happening. Probably the most important trait of a good trader is the ability to assess these facts and the ability to read human nature.

One myth that I hope this book dispels is the notion of trading being a glamorous industry full of limos, yachts, and the like. This is a stereotype that Hollywood has created for us. If all traders lived that type of lifestyle, then we would all be traders. Some do get there, but most lead relatively normal lives and come and go to work the same as anyone else. This book discusses all forms of traders and trading—exchange specialists, equity traders, debt traders, corporate bond traders, preferred stock traders, municipal traders, mortgage-backed security traders, international traders, swap traders, option traders, and futures traders. I hope that one of these fields will pique your interest.

Whether you decide to trade for yourself, or for someone else, remember you are talking about the deployment of money in order to make a profit. There are rules to be followed, but once you learn to "play" the game, profit should be your reward. Trading is not for everyone and not everyone can be a paid trader. To those who can, and enjoy it, there is a rich and rewarding career waiting for you. Good luck!

Introduction

SO YOU WANT TO BE A TRADER?

The majority of the people who come in contact with the securities industry have, from time to time, become fascinated with an occupation known as *trader*. Many in the industry have aspired to, or thought of aspiring to, become one. The position of trader has the aura of unbelievable amounts of pressure being placed on humans who have ice water running through their veins. The requirement for instantaneous reaction to news events, the buying and selling of issues, the maintenance of huge positions, the exhilaration of going home at night knowing that you have millions of dollars invested, the wheeling and dealing, all attract the fantasies of many.

Hollywood has added to this mystique with such movies as *Wall Street* and *Trading Places,* to name but a few. The news media has carried stories on some of the individuals who participate in this arena; in some cases, these wheelers and dealers have given the industry a "black eye." It is a shame too, as these individuals, with their inflated egos, feed the fires of the envious, making it difficult for the rest to operate in an environment that is healthy and proud.

To those who have wanted to become traders, their ambitions have, at times, been thwarted by the question, "Trade what?" The question is generally answered with the phrase, "You know, a trader!" It is interesting to watch the faces of the would-be traders as one starts to run down the list of issues being traded and toss in some generic terms to flavor the conversation.

THE TRADING CONCEPT

To answer the question "Trade what?", I've drawn up the following possible list of considerations:

1. Listed equities as a specialist on an exchange, or

2. Over-the-counter equities as an OTC trader.

How about trading

3. Debt instruments.

If you're interested, then how about trading

a. Corporate bonds, municipal bonds, or government bonds.

If undecided, add

b. Long-, intermediate-, or short-term issues.

If the decision made is for corporate long-term bonds, then consider *c.* Convertible, callable, sinking fund bonds, or

    d. Straight bonds.

Maybe some other product may be more appealing; what about trading

    4. Options (puts and calls).

If yes, then how about

    a. Stock, index, debt, or currency options.

If the answer to any of the four (a) selections is yes, then what about becoming

    b. An "upstairs" or "downstairs" trader.

While pondering the interest of being an options trader, let's examine the world of

    5. Futures, on

    a. Index, currency, commodities, or debt products.

    b. How about concentrating on one type or group of products such as soybean, soybean oil, and soybean meal.

If none of these appeal to you, maybe trading

    6. Money market instruments does.

How about trading

    a. Commercial paper (short-term debt of corporations),

    b. CDs (negotiable certificates of deposits including Euro CDs and Yankee CDs), or

    c. Banker acceptances, used in international trading.

    As you can see from the above list, there is a multitude of instruments available for trading, each with its own characteristics, and each requiring a special knowledge. The differences in these products are as different as the following story.

An individual goes into a restaurant and orders a Coke. The waiter says, "Cherry or regular?"

CUSTOMER: "Regular."
WAITER: "Classic or new?"
CUSTOMER: "New."
WAITER: "Diet or regular?"
CUSTOMER: "Diet."
WAITER: "Caffeine free or regular?"
CUSTOMER: "Never mind, make it a 7-Up."
WAITER: "Diet or regular?"

While all of the industry traders trade, what they trade is different. This book is aimed at the major issues traded and gives some insight into what traders look for in making their decisions. It must be remembered that there is much more to trading than this book will discuss, and there are types of trading that, due to their complexities, will not be explored. Complete books have been devoted to some of these theories and techniques already. If the reader, after completing this book, has some idea of becoming a trader in a particular security, then I suggest that you read books written on that one subject. Once you believe that you have a command of the subject, start to trade a *make-believe* inventory using pencil and paper, newspaper or other information sources. Try different strategies, but most importantly *don't use real money.*

Good luck!

Chapter 1

Trading in the Marketplace

INTRODUCTION TO TRADING

The world of the trader is one full of uncertainty. If the market was an orderly constant and all facets of trading were certainties, there would be no need for traders. As a matter of fact, there would be no need for a market. The price of any given issue would be undisputable, and as no changes could occur (everything being certain), the price would remain constant. However, the marketplace doesn't operate that way and because of the uncertainties that do exist, the price of an issue is always disputable. This dispute evolves into trading opportunities.

For example, the safest of all investments are *U.S. Treasury Bills* (T Bills). This instrument is backed by the full taxing power and strength of the U.S. government and is considered a *short-term instrument* (i.e., being exposed to market risk for a short period of time). If you were to purchase a six-month T Bill priced to yield 6.50%, at the end of that six-month period you would receive your initial investment plus interest computed to yield 6.50%. If the calculations for issues are so simple, as in this case of the T Bill, where is the uncertainty? The market is not an orderly constant and the calculations are rarely that simple.

What if interest rates were rising? The value of the T Bill would be falling, and if the investor had to *liquidate* (sell) before the maturity of the T Bill, the investor would incur a loss. As a trader, you would not want to hold an inventory position in this particular instrument at a time when interest rates were rising. What you would try to do is remain *flat* (i.e., not maintaining a position) and even try to sell ahead of buying hoping that the interest rate rise would cause you to sell at a higher price than what it would cost you to *cover* (buy back) the position later on.

As a trader, you could also hedge your position via the sale of *T Bill futures*. If interest rates do rise, the value of your issues will fall and your T Bill inventory will lose value. However, if your owned T Bills are losing value, your T Bill futures (which have been sold) are falling in value as well. If the positions were closed, the loss on the "physical" bills would be offset by the profit on the futures (you would be selling the long position below cost, but would be buying the futures back below the sale price).

As a trader, you could also be trading T Bills of different maturities against each other. T Bills are issued by the Federal Reserve Board through a weekly auction. In turn, the Bills mature on a weekly basis. If traders believe that interest rates are going to fall, they will look to buy the longest-term T Bill and "lock up" the higher rate for as long as possible. The demand will force the price up and, in turn, lower the yield while making the market in the near-term T Bills "soft" (a "firm" market is one where there is sufficient demand to support the price or market value. A "soft" market is one where any increase in supply (sellers) would cause a decrease in price), which would, in turn, lower the price causing the yield to rise. There is a value to time remaining in the various instruments and traders will trade on the market value difference between the different maturing T Bills.

T Bills are also part of a group of instruments known as *money market instruments*. These instruments are issued for a short period of time in a similar fashion to T Bills. These instruments, namely, *certificates of deposit* (CDs), *bankers acceptances* (BAs) and *commercial paper* (CPs) trade in the marketplace and, most importantly to a trader, they trade in a relationship to each other. As interest rates change, the relationship between the instruments changes. Traders will position themselves between these instruments and trade on the temporary market discrepancies.

We started this chapter off with the fact that the market is not perfect. To prove this, we briefly examined T Bills, "the safest of all investments." In this next section we will demonstrate some other trading possibilities.

TRADING IN THE INTERNATIONAL MARKETPLACE

Globalization is among the newest terms to be heard in the marketplace. The realization that what affects one country's economy has an effect on the world economy is becoming more prevalent as international trade and the use of different currencies and international investments continue to grow. The homogenization of our planet Earth is happening before our eyes. As such, the economies of Japan, Korea, Germany, England, Spain, Italy, and so on have a direct effect on the U.S. marketplace. By 1992, one of the Common Markets' marketplaces, now fragmented by denomination into different countries, will become the consolidated European market. The effect of this proposed united force has been discussed by the experts, but the true impact will not be known until the event happens.

The entire concept of globalization is not new. Concepts such as *twenty-four hour trading,* which originally sounded weird, is, in certain products, a reality and the concept is spreading to other instruments. Each morning, when Americans awake and turn on the radio, they hear where the London Gold "fix" is and where the Nikkei (Japanese (Tokyo) stock market index average) closed. People living in those countries find out about the American markets in the same fashion. Traders can, in some instances, trade between markets. They will trade on discrepancies between marketplaces or trade on trends following issues on each market as it opens and closes. Traders who are part of units that are active twenty-four hours a day pass their position from one trading location to the next. This resembles a relay race, but instead of a track, it spans the globe via telecommunication lines.

TRADING WITH INTEREST RATE FLUCTUATIONS

Many of the traded products react to interest rate changes. Some are more sensitive to this stimulus than others, but terms such as *rate of return, risk/reward,* and *time exposure,* to mention but a few, all relate to interest rates which in turn affect the market pricing mechanisms.

Traders are also affected by interest rates as the firm's cost to carry positions fluctuates with prevailing rates. Firms borrow money to pay for their security positions at a rate known as the *broker call rate.* Therefore, like any other business, the trader must out-earn this cost of carry, as well as the usual expenses such as heat, light, rent, and so on in order to be part of a profitable operation.

THE IMPORTANCE OF ESTABLISHING TRADING GUIDELINES

This brings us to perhaps the most overlooked part of being a trader, the core of the business, itself. A trader is constantly managing inventory which can fluctuate in value. That fluctuation will cause unrealized *profit* or *loss.* In order to create more profit and less loss, a trading firm should set down a few standard guidelines. Therefore, if you were managing traders, you would have to decide how much money (capital) should be allocated and used in the trading of:

A given issue;

A type of issue;

A sector of the market;

The multitude of different products;

The initial offering or secondary markets; and

The concentration or diversification in a specific product.

You should also determine:

What level of trade quality does your firm desire for its customers?

How much volatility does your firm's management desire of their traders?

Are you trading new or established products?

The answer, from a product control standpoint, depends on many factors such as:

What reputation do you want the firm to have or what reputation does the firm already have?

What are the firm's trade processing capabilities?

How much capital does the firm want to commit or can commit to the effort?

What are the firm's operating expense levels?

What are the firm's future plans?

Which segment of market participants do you want to call "customer"?

Perhaps, most important, what are the prospects for the market at this given point in time?

TRADING FOR PROFITS

Profitability is the magic word. As a trader, you and your firm should always be actively seeking new ways to improve profitability for both the firm and its clients. There is no yellow brick road, there is no easy street. Making a profit takes time and work. In the following section, we will discuss a few basic trading concepts which have proved profitable.

Activity and Profitability

The more active an issue, the better the apparent possibility for making a profit. The word "apparent" is used because the more active an issue, the more traders will participate; more traders mean more competition, resulting in less of a chance for profit.

A more dormant issue means less competition and a fewer number of competing traders. The less interest, the greater the position risk, resulting in a better chance for profit (or loss).

Dividends and Interest: Friends or Foes?

If the instrument pays dividends or interest, then the cost of carrying a position may be offset, in part or entirely, by the income distributed by the product(s) being traded. However, if the concept of being *short* (selling something that is not owned) is brought into the picture, then interest/dividends work against you.

Example: The concept of *short selling* is based on selling an issue you do not own with the expectation of buying it back later at a lower price. To accomplish the *short sale,* the particular issue is borrowed from someone or some entity who owns it and returned when the short sale is closed out. Another method of short selling is to temporarily *fail to deliver* (method by which the security is *not* delivered on settlement date) and use the *buying back issue* (a short sale results in the owing of stock. The position must eventually be closed out by buying in the stock previously sold) to satisfy the original sale (can be done for a short term). In both of these cases, interest or dividends will be working against the trader as the sale will bring with it the requirement to pay or owe the interest or dividend due on the borrowed or short security.

Interest Rates and the Cost of Carry

As we just saw, dividends and interest can cost your firm money. As such, the *cost of carry* sets the stage for many trading decisions. Remember, traders have the ability to earn profits or create losses in any type of market condition. Therefore, the cost of carry plays an important role in determining profit potential.

For example, if you were managing money, would you risk it in expectation of earning 15% if you could invest it safely for a rate of 5%? What about 10%? How about 12%? At what point does the *reward* justify the *risk*?

Let's follow this scenario further. Short-term rates (one year or less) are usually lower than long-term rates. However, due to aberrations in the marketplace, this relationship could narrow, be equal, or even reverse. When the latter occurs, the *yield curve* (charting of yields over time) is said to be a *convex curve*. Therefore, if you must borrow short-term funds to carry positions in long-term debt instruments, at what point does the cost of borrowing negate the value of trading long-term debt? While your trading may be profitable, the cost of carry is negating your profits.

Interest rates play an important part in determining fair market value of many nondebt instruments. For example, it plays a part in setting option premiums. As interest rates rise, so does the premium with all other factors being equal. Therefore, as the premium rises, the attractiveness of certain option strategies may diminish while other option strategies become more attractive.

Finally, for the equity market to be attractive to investors, there must be investment opportunities which will offer the potential of profit. As interest rates rise, money will usually flow from the equity market to the debt market. The effect of this would be a drop in stock prices. This, in turn, makes the equity marketplace less attractive which means traders are left with rising costs. They will, therefore, be trading in soft markets.

One way to overcome these two negatives is for the traders to widen the quotes, thereby earning more per buy/sell transaction.

Example: Romba Corp. is quoted at 35 1/8–1/4. The highest price a trader is willing to buy the stock at is 35 1/8, the lowest price at

which the trader will sell is 35 ¼. The difference between the bid
(35 ⅛) and the offer (35 ¼) is called the *spread.* In this case, the
spread is ⅛ of a point or $12.50 per 100 shares. Each time traders
buy stock from a *seller* and sell it to a *buyer,* they earn $12.50 per
100 shares. If the cost of carry forces traders to widen their quotes
to 35 ⅛–⅜, the *turnaround profit* is now ¼ of a point, or $25.00
per 100 shares. This could start a vicious spiral.

That is, as interest rates rise, quote spreads widen. As quote
spreads widen, participants in the particular marketplace seek out
instruments with better trading conditions. As they desert certain
issues, trading liquidity starts to "dry up," and the traders, having
fewer conduits to trade against, are reluctant to trade at those risk
levels. They, therefore, widen their quotes further to compensate
for the additional risk. This, in turn, drives more participants
away and so on.

It is important to "would-be traders" and to investors,
alike, that they completely understand the significance of the
quote spread. The more liquid the market, the more participants, resulting in a greater quantity of issues traded, thereby
instituting the need to change issue prices and to tighten quotes.
The tighter the quote, the more the market participants are willing to transact business. The greater the depth of the market, the
better the liquidity. It really is a chicken and egg scenario.

Example: You are an investor interested in buying shares of Pac-
quin Inv. The stock is quoted 24 ⅛–⅜. If the quote spread is ¼ of
a point, you have, upon purchase, lost $25.00 per 100 shares. (If
the quote never changes and if you are forced to liquidate, you
would receive 24 ⅛ or $25.00 less per 100 shares.) If Pacquin rose
5 points, the quote would probably be 29 ⅛–⅜. If you could sell it
at 29 ⅜, you would earn the 5-point profit. However, as you are
not the trader, you would probably sell the shares at 29 ⅛ for a
profit of 4 ¾ points. If, however, the stock fell 5 points, the quote
would probably be 19 ⅛–⅜, you would be selling at 19 ⅛ and not
19 ⅜ for a loss of 5 ¼. Remember, you buy from the trader's offer
and sell to the trader's bid.

The "give away" in the above example is the spread. As the spread widens, the ability to get into and out of a position becomes more expensive. This built-in cost affects your view of potential returns.

THE ROLES OF THE MARKET PARTICIPANTS

For a marketplace to be successful, there must be many participants—with many different interests. A dominant source will taint the marketplace. If the dominant source becomes a monopoly, the market will perish. By different interests, we are going further than the basic "someone wants to own" to "the stock is purchased from someone who wants to sell." In some instruments, we are referring to the existence of product relationships that have existed for time in memoriam; and when the relationships change, for whatever reason, traders will take positions.

Example: The thirty-year bonds of ZIP Company have "always" traded a quarter of a point below the thirty-year bonds of the POW Company. This relationship has existed for some time. Due to some market forces, this relationship changes. Traders begin to buy one issue and sell the other one, waiting for the relationship to be reestablished and then close the position. When (and if) the correction occurs, the traders will lock in a profit.

Example: The cost to carry a certain commodity future is $X\%$. Because of active trading in the next deliverable month, the market price has moved so that the difference between the different contract month prices has inflated (or depressed). As the price of one month against another is greater/less than the cost of carry, traders will buy one, sell the other, and wait for the market to neutralize (assuming all other conditions are equal).

In both of the above examples, the trader's risk is that the "temporary abnormality" may not be temporary and may not be an abnormality. At worst, it may be a harbinger of things to come and, therefore, the trader is actually on the "wrong side" of the market, incurring a loss.

In very heavily traded markets, market makers (traders) earn profits by *trading the spread* and following trends. If the market price of a given issue is rising, traders will buy the issue and try to sell it at the next trading graduation.

Example: A future is trading at a quote of 140.55–.60. A trader would buy the future contract at 140.60 and immediately offer it at 140.65. While this type of trading may look like an easy way to earn money, buying at the wrong time and/or the cost of trade processing could "eat up" whatever profits were earned.

TRADERS AND THE DIFFERENT MARKETPLACES

Traders in the various instruments position themselves differently in their respective marketplaces. Traders need different sources of orders to function. *Public, institutional portfolio managers,* and *hedgers* form the first tier. Each can be divided into subgroups:

Public Traders. This includes the speculator, the investor for capital appreciation, and the investor for dividends/ interest.

Institutional Portfolio Managers. These are individuals who maintain security positions in attempting to achieve certain prearranged or preestablished criteria. Among these criteria are growth, income, and safety.

Hedgers. A hedger's main concern is the relationship between products and trade on differences. The adoptability of the product to the hedger's need will determine the amount of interaction in the marketplace and therefore the amount or type of order flow.

Let us focus on one product to show the interaction of different traders and different interests.

Trading U.S. Treasury Bond (T Bond) Futures

Different participants in the T Bond future market include:

Individuals trying to lock in a specific interest rate now that would be applicable later on.

Individuals trying to unlock or offset a current rate.

Individuals trying to take advantage of long-term rates over the short term.

T Bond traders attempting to hedge their present positions or set up positions for a later date.

Mortgage-backed security traders who trade current or forward positions to establish a hedge.

Future traders who trade on the floor of the Chicago Board of Trade could be:

Spreaders. They trade one maturing future month against another month or against another product (i.e., a "floor trader" that buys the nearest month T Bond future and sells a further out month against that position).

Scalpers. They buy then sell or sell then buy quickly, trying to take advantage of the particular future's spread. Does not usually maintain a position of any size but will operate between the quote in trading strategies.

Interproduct Traders. They trade one product against another. For example, they buy (selling) the T Bond future while simultaneously selling (buying) the T Bill future.

Hedgers. Hedgers lay off one product's risk through the use of another product. A T Bond futures trader may use T Bond options to cover or curtail some of the risk in the futures position. For example, buying T Bond futures and buying T Bond put options would protect the trader if the price of T Bonds fell.

(These products will be explained in more detail later on.)

What is so important about the above list and so critical to the marketplace is that certain participants may be acquiring those T Bond future contracts for the same reason(s) others are selling (i.e., *hedging* positions). No one group dominates the market and, therefore, many are willing to participate because "big or small," they perceive that they are being fairly represented.

Another product that lends itself to many situations are stock options. A call option gives the owner the privilege of buying the underlying stock. A put grants the owner the privilege of selling. Apply this concept to an interesting stock such as International Business Machines (IBM) and an electrifying marketplace evolves.

Individuals, for example, who own the stock can sell calls against the position to increase income. Individuals who believe the stock may rise in market value can buy calls or sell (write) puts. Those who think the stock may do the reverse would buy a put or write a call. Still others will use one call against another or a put against a put in attempting to achieve certain goals.

Traders in option products are cognizant of the previously mentioned strategies, plus many others. They, therefore, trade in and out of positions in attempting to offset these transactions. What a trader in options does and how options trade are introduced in a later section.

Many who are familiar with the market will, at times, refer to it as if it were alive and/or part of the animal kingdom. For example, in referring to an index value one may hear, "she is up 3.53" or "the market is dead," or "the market is nervous," or "it is jumpy." As part of the animal kingdom, you'll hear "who killed whom," "he made a killing," "she rode the stock," "he got belted," the stock "fell out of bed," this stock could be "the sleeper of the year," and, of course, "look at 'er go," "they saw me coming," "the market is weak, sick, strong," and so on. Many of these terms actually refer to the participants in the market. The participants, themselves, may not be sure of its direction or are "watching for down (up) signals." Therefore, the market or issue is soft meaning it will fall in value with the slightest selling pressure. It is important to understand this concept, because a strong stock may fall in value in a weak or soft market.

The reverse is true, also. A weak stock may, in fact, rise in a strong or firm market. It is important for a trader or any market participant to understand the emotion or current psychological mind set of the market populace.

Example: If two major banks increase the prime lending rate by ¼ of a point, it may or may not affect the bond market. If it does affect the market, it may cause bond prices to fall in value or it may cause bond prices to rise. The market's mind set will determine the impact. If the rise in the prime rate came as a surprise, then bond prices would probably fall. If the change in the prime rate was expected, the market price of the instruments would have already taken it into account and, therefore, wouldn't change. Finally, if the marketplace had expected a greater increase, say a ½-point rise in the prime rate, then price would rise as debt instruments have probably been "oversold."

Of course, sometimes the banks, which are first to announce rate changes, will alter the "change" as other banks adjust their rates. For example, two major banks announce a ¼ of a point rise in the prime rate. Several other major banks follow in a day or two with a larger increase. Eventually, the initial two banks will fall into line. If the market anticipated the ¼ of a point change, then the announcement by the first banks would be a nonevent. However, if the marketplace expected more or less of an increase it could very well take adjustment action and then have to readjust when the other banks make their changes to the prime rate. As a trader involved with fixed income or other interest rate-sensitive issues, this type of market situation could produce a profit or a loss depending on how the market conditions affected the trader's position or how well the trader anticipated the banks' activity.

Traders in any product must be fully cognizant of what is happening not only in their products, but in other product areas which have some direct or indirect relation to them.

As mentioned earlier in the book, traders watch certain indicators and try to assess the effect these "road markers" may have on the prices of their respective products. This practice is more complicated than it may first appear, as not only must the trader understand the result of a road marker itself, but must analyze what effect the indicator has in light of other indicators and whether the market already compensated for the event.

One of the major factors in our economy is interest rates which affect all kinds of borrowings. Interest rates, therefore, have an effect on most of the products traded. As such, traders follow any indicator that may foretell future interest rate changes. One of the most obvious is the U.S. Treasury Auction, one of which is conducted on a weekly basis. At first, bond traders anticipate what the level of interest will be for the new instruments and then they adjust their positions, if needed, so that they are where they want to be when the actual auction takes place.

For example, T Bills are auctioned every Monday. The week-to-week rates give a strong indication as to which way interest rates are heading. The difference from one week to the next can be insignificant or a major move. The important item is its movement and, therefore, an insignificant move is still a move, and when compared to previous levels, forms an important part of the interest rate change.

At the writing of this book, three-month T Bills were auctioned at 6.89%. The previous week's auction was 6.88%. Obviously an insignificant move. A year ago, the rate was 5.98%. Is the move still insignificant?

In anticipating this week's auction, traders who thought the rate would be lower than the previous weeks would have gone into the market and bought debt issues anticipating a rise in prices. Remember, as interest rates rise, bond prices fall and yield rises, and vice versa. Any trader expecting lower rates would have been incorrect, as rates actually rose. Due to the slight movement, those traders "got off lucky" as they could "unwind" the position at a small loss. Traders who estimated the correct movement made a small (very small) profit and can trade out of the positions.

To guesstimate interest rate movement, traders watch various indicators. Some follow "the money supply" as one of these indicators. There are three levels of money supply—M1, M2, and M3.

M1 is composed of currency in circulation, traveler's checks issued, and checking accounts including NOW accounts. M2 includes M1 plus savings deposits, money market deposit accounts, money market funds, overnight repos, and overnight Eurodollars commitment. M3 includes M2 plus large time deposits, longer-term repos, Eurodollar commitments, and institutional money funds.

Followers of the money supply watch these figures for indications of interest rate moves. For example, if the money supply grows too quickly, it could mean that an inflationary trend is developing. This could mean higher interest rates as the *Fed* (Federal Reserve) tries to curb money growth. The Fed could raise the discount rate (the rate the Fed charges banks for refinancing) making it more expensive for banks to borrow. In addition, as the money supply grows, the demand for money also grows which in turn causes banks to raise their rates. As banks' rates rise, debt instruments coming to market must offer higher rates to attract investors. Those interest-rate sensitive instruments that are in the marketplace must offer higher yields to stay market competitive, so their market value falls. Drops in M1, M2, or M3 could be indicative of the reverse.

Another meaningful figure is the *Gross National Product* (GNP). As a leading indicator of the economy, its growth or contraction describes the health of the economy. The rate of growth or contraction is equally important. As a trader, you would expect the market(s) to adjust for the GNP's direction. You trade against the guesstimated amount of impact that this figure will have on the market.

An indicator which has a strong impact on the market is the *trade deficit figure*. As it is of so much concern, professionals, as well as nonprofessionals, in the marketplace try to anticipate what the "new" trade figure will be by adjusting their trading or inventory positions and/or trading strategies in anticipation.

The trade deficit figure represents a major portion of the amount that the federal government must finance. This borrowing draws or absorbs funds from the marketplace. As the deficit grows, the federal government needs more funds to finance itself. This demand could cause interest rates to rise. As the deficit shrinks, the government needs less funds to finance and therefore there is less demand.

Another leading indicator is the *New York Stock Exchange's* (NYSE's) *short interest figures*. This represents the securities listed on the Exchange which have been sold short and therefore they are the amount of each security's short position that exists and how it has changed from the previous period. It includes the number of shares short per security and the overall short position amount.

Traders watch this report for two reasons. First, as the figures grow, the short position represents potential demand as the short sellers will eventually have to cover or close out their positions. Traders try to analyze why the overall figure is changing. For example, are the short sellers truly foretelling of things to come? If the short sale figures rise, does it mean the market or the individual securities will fall in value? Are the "shorts" growing because the market is perceived as being too "high"? Are the short sellers just plain paranoid?

Second, in using these various indicators, individuals must be cognizant of new products or strategies that may affect the indicator. With the introduction of derivative products such as options, "short sales" are not short sales in the parochial sense of the word. For example, an option strategy used by some professional traders is known as a *reversal*. This strategy utilizes a three-legged position consisting of a short sale of stock, the purchase of a call, and the writing (selling) of a put on that issue. The long call and written put neutralize the market risk from the short sale.

Therefore, in the short interest figure of the NYSE, short sales from strategies like the above, must be considered in evaluation. For the most part, they are *not* predicting market movement or future guesstimates. In other words, the greater the percentage of short sales caused by nonmarket related strategies, the less meaningful the indicator.

Perhaps the most stimulating argument in the industry is that of the *chartist*, or technical analyst, against those that do not believe in charts at all. The world of the chartist is different from just plain market watching. The history of trading prices is recorded and trends are developed. It is these trends that are watched carefully. As the pattern develops, repetition is studied with investment or trading decisions based on interpretations of the charts.

For example, a stock has traded from 25 to 45 over time,

Figure 1.1.   Chartist's Drawing of Stock Trends.

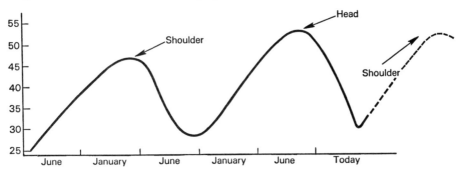

then went back down to 28, then up to 50, then down to 30, and now is on its way up (see Figure 1.1).

Based on Figure 1.1 (overly simplistic as it may be), the stock appears to be an attractive buy. It appears to be entering its third cycle or the second shoulder of a *head and shoulder trend.* The figure reveals a series of movements: a shoulder, then a head, and then the second shoulder appears to be forming.

Another terminology used by chartists is *support and resistance* levels. Chartists believe that when a stock falls to a certain level, it becomes an attractive buy and buyers enter the market developing demand, which prevents the price from falling further. However, as the price rises, profit taking sets in, which brings sellers in, creating supply, and which prevents the price from rising.

In Figure 1.2, the stock is trading at about 39. A chartist would estimate where the next resistance level is, say 43, and

Figure 1.2.   Example of Support and Resistance.

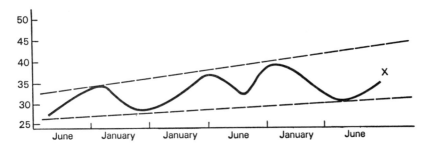

where the next support level is, say 33. At its current price, a chartist may feel that the stock may not be as attractive as it would be if the stock broke through 43. The chartist would attempt to determine where the next resistance level would be, maybe 50 or 55.

It's important to remember that no one technique, data source, or theory works all the time. However, depending on what is being traded, a trader must know which has relevancy to the product and how it is interpreted and applied.

As mentioned earlier, not everyone follows or believes in chartists. For example, a very proficient trader that I know follows charts but does not believe in them. Her philosophy is to trade against what the chartists are preparing to do.

For example, if the stock market grows weak and investors in that marketplace begin to sell their securities, where will they invest their newly freed-up funds next? They could put these proceeds in savings accounts, money market funds, or the bond market. It would appear that when the expectation of "making a killing" turns into a loss of capital, an 8% return from a fairly safe investment becomes attractive. As such, traders in money market instruments (i.e., T Bills, commercial paper, certificates of deposit, and so on), intermediate-term instruments (i.e., corporate and U.S. T Notes), and long-term instruments (T Bonds, corporate bonds, and municipal bonds) adjust their positions in anticipation of market action.

It is this anticipation that requires the special tuning of a professional trader. One knows that an event is going to have some type of impact on the product traded. But how much of an impact is critical for profit or a healthy "bottom line"?

We have already discussed the cost of carry and other related expenses. Suppose you, as a trader, anticipate that some event could have a positive impact on a stock for which you are a market maker. At the present time, 25% of your money line is invested in that stock, the remaining 75% is invested in four other securities in which you are also a market maker. What would you do, what action would you take? Here is a list of considerations:

1. You already have the greatest percentage of trading funds tied up in this security.

2. The more resources you put in this issue, the less you can devote to other "any other" issues.

3. If you keep status quo, you may be missing an opportunity to increase your trading revenue on which your compensation is determined.

4. In order for you to increase your participation in the issue under consideration, you must liquidate some of your other positions. If you did, would you have a realized profit or loss based on current market values?

5. What if you decide to take a loss as described in 4, and there is little or no effect on the issue under consideration after the event happened?

6. Worse yet, what if this issue under consideration doesn't increase in value but the issue(s) that you sold at a loss does?

7. Regardless of the above, what "condition" is the market in? What is the possibility that the overall market, as well as the issue in question, may fall in value? Are any of the other securities that you hold in inventory better able to resist a downturn?

By the time you read this far in this section and think about the above seven steps, as a trader, you would have missed the market opportunity.

SUMMARY

In conclusion, this brief chapter has introduced some of the elements that go into being a good trader. Some of the facets presented are not considered when people think of becoming traders. Other facets are misunderstood. What we have looked at is only the "tip of the iceberg" as to what it takes to be a good trader.

However, this chapter was not meant to dissuade anyone from becoming a trader. Many of the areas discussed will become second nature over time to a new trader and some areas are not applicable in all products. The purpose of this chapter was to widen the horizons of some who perceive trading as a buy/sell, get rich quick occupation.

We will now begin to focus on instrument traders, and how traders of those instruments attempt to be successful in trading for profit.

Chapter 2

Orders

WHAT IS AN ORDER?

It is important that you understand the types of orders that are used in the marketplace. An *order* is an explicit instruction to the individual responsible for the execution. That individual is not a mindreader and must, by established rules of the respective marketplace, follow the instructions of each order. Orders that are obviously incorrect will be challenged; orders that fall within the panorama of legally permitted orders will be accepted and the resulting execution, or lack thereof, is the responsibility of the executioner.

TIME CONSTRAINTS

There are two types of time constraints—*day* or *good-til-canceled.* Day orders expire at the end of the day of entry if they are not executed. Good-til-canceled orders remain in force until they are either executed or canceled.

You must remember that an order represents an intent to implement a plan of action. As time passes, situations change and what appeared to be a good situation on one day, may now be different. The perception of the market may have adjusted since the order was placed. Any one of a hundred different factors, directly or indirectly affecting the situation, may have happened causing the order's constraint to be satisfied, which means the execution will take place when it may no longer be advantageous to do. All orders may be canceled before execution takes place.

PRICE CONSTRAINTS

Market Orders

A *market order* accepts the best price available. *Buy market orders* accept the quote's offer. *Sell market orders* are executed against the quote's bid. The quote is only valid for the number of shares comprising the quote (the size).

Example: The quote is 42 1/8–1/2, 8 × 5

Translation: There are 800 shares bid at 42 1/8 and 500 shares offered at 42 1/2.

These are two important facts to remember about quotes and sizes:

1. The quote reflects a market condition at a period of time. The "older" a quote, the less likely that it is still valid. It is always possible that as you read the quote on some vendor's screen, it is in the process of being changed.

2. Size is time critical. If still valid, the bid can absorb a sale of 800 shares, whereas the offer can absorb a purchase of 500 shares. Orders for quantities greater than this would be filled partially, or in their entirety, at a price higher (for buys) or lower (for sells) than the established quote.

Limit Orders

Limit orders set the maximum price that a purchaser is willing to pay or the minimum price a seller is willing to accept.

Buy limit orders entered below the current offer cannot be filled unless, or until, someone is willing to sell at that price. Buy limit orders entered below the current bid cannot be executed as there are buyers willing to pay more. Finally, this type of order entered above the current offer can be executed up to, and including, the buy limit order's price.

Example: The quote is 42 1/8–1/2. If a buy order is entered at 42 1/4, the bid would change to 42 1/4, as the new order is willing to accept a higher price than the previous bid.

If a buy order is entered below the bid, this would mean having to wait for the market price to drop through the higher bid(s) which would have to be filled or canceled before the new bid can be entertained.

If a buy order is entered above the offer, this would mean execution at the offer and, if the share quantity demanded, up to the limit price.

Sell limit orders operate in a similar fashion. Sell limits entered above the current offer cannot be executed until the market price increases and fills all offers priced below the limit price. Offers made below the current offer but above the highest bid will become the new offer. Sell limit orders entered below the current bid will be executed against the bids down to, and including, the limit price if the share quantity of one order demands it.

Note: Trades executed in the over the counter (OTC) market are sometimes executed on a principal basis. In this manner of execution, the execution price includes a markup (buy) or a markdown (sell).

That is, if the quote is 42 1/8– 1/2 and the buy limit price is 42 1/2, the order may not be executed because the price would not permit the dealer's markup. If the buyer pays 42 1/2 and the seller is expecting to receive 42 1/2 per share, there is no room for the markup or dealer's profit. If the dealer can find a seller below 42 1/2, say 42 1/4, the dealer would buy the stock at 42 1/4 and sell it to the buyer at 42 1/2, thereby making the 1/4-point markup. Therefore, limit orders, especially good-til-canceled limit orders must be used with care. Over-the-counter and exchange trading methodologies will be discussed in Chapter 4.

Short Sales

It is easy to understand the strategy needed when a security appears to be rising in value—buy it! But what if the perception of the stock is that it is going to decrease in value? If the security could be sold first and bought back at a later date at a lower price, a profit would be achieved. This is known as a *short sale*. To complete this process, stock must be borrowed and used for the delivery against the sale. Later when it is bought back, the security is returned to the lender. The difference between the sale price and the later purchase is the resulting profit or loss. During the period of time that the short sale is in force, however, the borrower of the stock owes the lender any dividends paid by the corporation.

In Securities and Exchange Commission-regulated stock and bond exchanges, trades are recorded and these recordings are known as *ticks*. Under the 1934 Securities Exchange Act, which is part of the federal regulations governing the securities industry, short sales can only be effected on an uptick or a zero uptick. What this means is that one can only sell stocks or bonds short if the sale is higher than the previous sale (an uptick) or equal to the previous sale but higher than the last different sale (zero uptick). For example, let's say sales occur at 36– 1/2, 5/8, 5/8, 5/8, 1/2, 1/2. The first 5/8 sale is higher than the previous sale making it an uptick. The second and third 5/8 sales are the same as the previous sale but higher than the last different sale, making them zero uptick sales. Short sales could only be effected on these conditions.

Stop Orders

Stop orders are protection orders and have no standing until their price is reached or passed. *Buy stop orders* are entered above the current market; *sell stops* are entered below. A stop order becomes a market order when its price is reached or passed.

Example: With the quote 42 1/8–42 1/2 a short seller sold stock at 42 1/8 and wants to be protected against a rise in the market price. The seller is willing to be exposed to a five-point loss. Therefore, an order is entered to buy 100 shares at 47 1/8 *stop.* This is a memorandum order which will become a market order if the stop price of 47 1/8 is reached or passed by the market price.

Note: if the word "stop" was not included on the order, it would be a limit order to buy stock as high as 47 1/8. With the quote 42 1/8–1/2 the order could be executed at 42 1/2 on a 47 1/8 limit, which is not the short seller's intention. The short seller wants to buy the stock only if it reaches the price of 47 1/8 or higher. Therefore, a stop order is entered.

Stop orders are also entered by purchasers of stock. A customer buying stock at 42 1/2 would like to minimize exposure. Assume five points is what the buyer wants to risk. The individual would enter a sell stop order at 37 1/2. If the market value of the stock falls 37 1/2 or below, the stop order becomes a market order and is executed on the then prevailing bid.

Note: Stop orders set a limit that the market must reach. When that limit has been reached, the order then becomes a market order. This does not guarantee an execution at that price, though.

Example: An individual bought stock at 42 1/2 and entered a good-til-canceled sell stop order at 37 1/2. Let's assume the market value in the stock falls to 38 at the close of a given day. Since the criteria of the order (37 1/2) has not been satisfied, the order will not be executed. Assume the next day the stock opens for trading at 35, with the quote 34³/₄–35. The stop order would be executed against the best prevailing bid(s) (depending on order and quote size) and then it would be executed at 34³/₄.

Stop orders are usually good-til-canceled (GTC) orders. They are entered into in order to protect a position, so they should be canceled when the protection is no longer needed. If this step is forgotten, the GTC order may be executed long after the situation that it was entered into to protect has been closed out.

Not Held Orders

To ensure that orders are executed on a timely basis and in accordance with uniform procedures, the various marketplaces have rules that must be followed by the participants. Occasionally, the originator of an order may perceive that it is prudent not to confine the order to these execution procedures. For example, let's assume the quote and size is 42¹/₄–³/₄, 8 × 10 (800 shares bid × 1,000 shares offered) and the originator wants to acquire 3,000 shares "at the market." The executioner of the order would have to buy the 1,000 shares offered at 42³/₄ and then continue executing the order against higher and higher offers until the order is filled.

After the execution is completed, the market price of the security would return to its fair value, causing the buyer of the 3,000 shares to, in effect, overpay for the stock. On the other hand, the buyer of 3,000 shares could enter a limit order at 42³/₄. One thousand shares would be "filled" at 42³/₄ and the 2,000 shares would become the new bid. The buyer would then have to wait for sellers to enter the market. Should anyone else want to purchase stock, all they would have to do is bid ¹/₈ of a point higher (42⁷/₈) and the originator of the 3,000-share order would lose the bid to the new buyer.

To suit the needs of the 3,000-share buyer, a special type of order, known as a *not held* (NH) order was developed. This order releases the order executioner from time and sale accountability as required by the marketplace rules. Therefore, the executioner can go into the marketplace when the quote and size is 42¹/₄–³/₄,

8×10 and buy 1,000 shares at 42¾ and then stand back allowing the market to reform again. Trades may take place, which the buyer would have been entitled to, if the order was not marked NH. When the executioner is of the opinion that more trades can be executed without upsetting the balance, additional shares are acquired, then the executioner pulls back again.

Another advantage to a not held order is that it gives another executioner an opportunity to advise the potential seller of the perceived buy order. (i.e., "I think there may be a buy order for a couple of thousand shares. If you're interested, I will speak to the broker.") If the owner of the stock is comfortable with the price, the executioner representing the seller will query the executioner representing the buyer, and a trade would occur.

The benefit to the marketplace is:

1. The buyer has not overpaid for the stock;

2. The seller received a fair price;

3. The fair value in the marketplace has not been upset.

Strategy Orders: All or None, Fill or Kill, and Immediate or Cancel Orders

All or None Orders. All or none (AON) orders inform the executioner that all of the order must be filled or the originator does not have to accept anything. Therefore, in accepting the order, the executioner is obligated to "fill it." If the executioner cannot complete the order, the executioner "owns" the portion of the order that has been completed. Therefore, in accepting such an order, the executioner must use his or her best market judgment.

Fill or Kill Orders. Fill or kill (FOK) orders simply state "fill the entire order immediately or cancel it." For example, the quote and size of RAM is 42⅛–¾, 20×30 (2,000 shares bid $\times$ 3,000 shares offered). An order is entered to buy 2,000 shares *FOK*. As there is an ample quantity offered, the order would be filled. If, however, the order was for 4,000 shares, the entire order would be canceled.

Immediate or Cancel Orders. Immediate or cancel (IOC) orders instruct the executioner to execute as much as possible immediately and cancel the remainder. In the above example, had the order been for 2,000 shares, it would have been filled. If, however, the order was for 4,000 shares, the executioner would have accepted the 3,000 offered and the remaining 1,000 shares wanted would be canceled.

Other Types of Orders

There are other types of orders, some of which pertain to certain products. For example, in some mortgage-backed security issues, there are orders for *known pools* or *yield equivalents.* In the world of options there are *spreads, straddles, combos,* and so on. It is important to note, however, that regardless of what the order is conveying, it is doing so through the use of a minimum amount of written instruction. These abbreviated documents must use commonly accepted terminology.

SUMMARY

An order is a communique that tries to accomplish a desired result. All orders and resulting executions fall under the rules and regulations of the respective marketplace. It is, therefore, imperative to understand how the marketplace operates in order to understand how your order will be handled. For example, while a market order accepts the "best" price, the definition of "the best price" differs from marketplace to marketplace. And while the highest bid and lowest offer, which represent limit orders, comprise the quote, the execution of these orders is dependent on the policies and practices of that marketplace.

As a professional trader working with other professionals, you may develop types of orders and some variations which will be used but will have no legal standing in the marketplace. These variations are accepted between the two professional parties. For example, good for a period of time orders or instructions to participate but don't initiate are not recognized orders. No marketplace acknowledges orders such as "Good thru 11:00 A.M." The

order is either a day or good-til-canceled. However, two professionals working together, agreeing to these terms will employ
such instructions to try to achieve desired results.

Several forms of orders have been reviewed in this chapter. It
is important to note that the responsibility for the order lies with
the originator and the eventual executioner. The more restrictive
the order, the less the chance of execution. Also, remember, that
an order entering a marketplace is entering a live, vibrant, and
constantly changing environment. What appeared doable one
moment may not be available the next. It is for this reason that
most traders try to get in and out of positions as quickly and
simply as possible. They use constraints only when they are abso-
lutely necessary. As you participate in the marketplace, regardless of your capacity, remember what your primary objectives are
and use those orders that will give you the *greatest flexibility* in
achieving them.

Chapter 3

The Exchange Specialist

THE SPECIALIST'S FUNCTION

The term *specialist* is applied to individuals who perform a market-making type function on some exchanges. To be permitted to transact business on the exchange floor, the individual must own or lease a *seat*. The term "seat" is synonymous with the term "membership."

As most of this book is concerned with the over-the-counter market (OTC) as well as the traders and products that are its part and parcel, it will be beneficial to take time out to discuss both types of marketplaces.

Trading in Both Marketplaces

Exchanges are described as *auction markets,* whereas the over-the-counter market is described as a *negotiated market.* On an exchange, for example, the highest bid and lowest offer have precedence or have "the floor." The bid or offer must be satisfied before any transactions can take place above that existing offer or below that existing bid. Since the OTC is a negotiated market, transactions based on the best overall or average price "could take place above the best offer or below the best bid with nothing being owed to the market makers of the then standing bid or offer."

Example: The quote and size of Racheal First National on an exchange is 38 $\frac{1}{4}$–$\frac{3}{4}$, 2 × 10.

Translation: The highest bid is $38.25 per share. The lowest offer is $38.75 per share. There are 200 shares comprising the bid and 1,000 shares composing the offer, ergo, 38 $\frac{1}{4}$–$\frac{3}{4}$, 2 × 10. If an order is received to sell 500 shares at the market, 200 of the shares would have to be sold to the bidder and the remainder at the next highest bid. On the other hand, in the over-the-counter market, given the same situation, the 500 shares would be sold to the "dealer" who would be willing to buy all 500 shares at the best overall price with no obligation on the part of the seller to satisfy the then existing highest bid.

The exchange markets are also considered *agency* or *broker markets,* whereas the over-the-counter market is considered a principal or dealer market. What this means is that public orders going to an exchange floor are represented by a *floor broker* who charges a floor commission for his execution service. The broker is acting as an agent. In the over-the-counter market, however, the order is "traded" against a firm acting as principal or market maker. The public *buys* against or from the firm or dealer and the public *sells* against or to the firm or dealer. There are some exceptions to this generality but in the majority of cases, however, it is true.

Example: Assume a customer wants to purchase 100 shares of Cameo stock and enters a limit order at 21. The translation is that the client does not want to pay more than $21 per share per 100 shares. Another client is looking to sell 100 shares of Cameo "at the market." The translation being, the seller is willing to accept the current bid.

In the dealer market or the over-the-counter market, the best quote at this particular moment of time is 20⅞–21⅛, 5 × 5. The dealer holding the buy limit order must find a seller who is willing to offer stock below $21 per share in order for that buyer's firm to acquire the stock and *mark it up* so that they can generate revenue from the transaction without violating the customer's $21 limit. With the current quote at 20⅞–21⅛, this order cannot be filed (executed) on a principal basis. The sell market order can be filed, however. It would be executed at 20⅞, less *markdown* (say ½ point) for the seller's firm's revenue and the client would receive 20⅜, or $2,037.50 per 100 shares.

Given a similar situation on an exchange with the quote at 20⅞–21⅛, the broker representing the buy order would have to bid the 100 shares at 21. As this bid is the highest bid, it would "take the floor" and the quote would become 21–⅛. When the sell market order arrived, it would be executed against the buying customer order. The execution would take place at 21. The buyer would be paying $21 per share plus commission; the seller would receive $21 less commission.

The above example highlights some of the differences between the OTC (dealer) market and the exchange (broker) markets. Half of every trade occurring on the OTC market requires a dealer, whereas the public can trade against each other on an exchange.

The Specialist's Trading Methodology

If the public can trade against each other on the exchanges, what do specialists do for a living? The primary responsibility of a specialist is to maintain a *fair and orderly market*. This phrase does not imply price control or price fixing. It does mean price continuity, which is accomplished by sometimes trading for their own account and risk when imbalances occur in trading. Specialists also execute public limit orders entrusted to them.

The specialist trading methodology is used on several equity and option exchanges. The different exchange rules governing their trading activity are similar to the differences evolving from the products traded. For example, when a stock transaction takes place on an exchange, it is known as a *tick* (named after the old, and I mean old, ticker tape machines). Certain trading rules are based on the tick. Options, as a derivative product, do not use ticks as a basis for trading rules.

WHO IS A SPECIALIST?

Who, or what, is a specialist? The term refers to an individual or a unit. For example, Ararey & Co. is a *specialist unit.* One of the firm's principals, Tip Ararey, is one of the firm's specialists. The firm may or may not conduct other types of business, but for the purpose of this book, they are only specialists.

HOW A SPECIALIST UNIT TRADES

The specialist unit operates on the floor of an exchange. The exchange, which is owned by its members, has various types of member committees. One of these committees if the *Specialist Allocation Committee.* This committee is comprised of members representing various segments of the industry. It is this group's responsibility to "allocate" available issues to the most deservant of the applying specialist units.

The individual exchanges maintain surveillance reports and various types of performance criteria that each specialist unit must satisfy. The performance ratings are developed from questionnaires or other types of surveys completed by members, and from reviews of how the unit satisfied criteria that are formulated by exchange committees. The surveillance history is developed by the exchange staff, who are responsible for monitoring trading activity. These employees are also responsible for investigating trading complaints originating from different industry sources.

When an issue becomes available for listing, in order to obtain the issue, specialist units must apply to the Specialist Allocation Committee. A rather lengthy form is completed by the unit giving relevant facts as to why the unit believes it deserves the issue, what resources will be available, how much capital the unit has available, and so on. The committee (armed with the ratings, performance data, and so forth) interviews each applying unit and then, usually in closed sessions, allocates the issue to one of the applicants. (Exchanges also permit units that did not receive the issue through allocation to compete. These units are known as *competing specialists.*) While this does happen occasionally, the "battle" is usually short lived with the more aggressive specialist quickly emerging the winner.

If the specialist unit continues to perform in an exemplary fashion, and as long as the unit's capital will allow, the unit will continue to apply for new listings. However, this apparent franchise has strict limitations on the specialist's ability to trade the specialty issue. Remember, this is an auction market, not a dealer market. For example, the specialist should avoid:

1. Liquidating all or substantially all of a position by selling at prices below the last different price or by purchasing stock above the last different price.

2. Failing to maintain a fair and orderly market during liquidation.

3. Participating as a dealer in opening a stock in such a manner as to upset the public balance of supply and demand as reflected by market and limit orders pending execution.

This last item is of major importance to the reader's understanding of the specialist's role on the exchange. Therefore, let's review this *opening process.*

OPENING A STOCK

It is before the opening of business on May 11, 19xx. Orders to buy and sell are being received at the *specialist post.* A specialist post is a location on the exchange floor where the specialist trades the particular product. As a "listed" product will only trade at one location on the exchange floor, all members having an interest in trading this product must go to this location or post to trade. Our specialist, Tip Ararey, has a good-til-canceled order file (previously entered orders) to which he is adding the new orders (both market and limit) being received. These orders are added either electronically to the specialist's order file, or are mentally stored as they are announced by the brokers. At the opening of trading, the specialist has the following limit order in his specialty stock for the account of C. B. Ranji:

Buy Shares	Price	Sell Shares
700	49 $1/4$	—
200	49 $3/8$	100
300	49 $1/2$	400
500	49 $5/8$	300
100	49 $3/4$	500

Let's assume, for this example, that the specialist has equal shares of buy and sell market orders.

If the decision was made to open the stock for trading at 49 $3/4$, the specialist would have to execute the 100 share buy order and *all* the sell orders when the "lowest offer has the floor." Therefore, the specialist could not "open" the stock at $3/4$ without "filling" the $5/8$, $1/2$, and $3/8$ stock that is for sale for a total of 1,300 shares. To do this, the specialist would have to buy 1,200 shares for his own account.

If the stock was opened for trading at 49 $5/8$, the buy orders at $5/8$ and $3/4$ would be executed for a total of 600 shares. The sell orders at $5/8$, $1/2$, and $3/8$ also would be executed for a total of 800 shares. The buy orders below $5/8$ would not be entitled to an execution and neither would the sell orders above $5/8$. In this case, the specialist would have to purchase 200 shares to satisfy the imbalance.

If the stock was opened for trading at 49 $1/2$, buy orders at $1/2$, $5/8$, and $3/4$ would have to be filled for a total of 900 shares. Sell orders of 500 shares (orders with limits of $3/8$ and $1/2$) would be executed against the buys. The specialist would have to be willing to sell 400 shares to satisfy the imbalance. All other factors being equal, the specialist would have to open the stock at 49 5/8 in order to minimize his participation.

To this equation, now add market orders where the buys and sells do not equal. These orders, when added to the pending limit orders could result in a completely different picture. Refer back to the example. Suppose that besides the limit orders pictured, the specialist was holding buy market orders for 2,000 shares and sell market orders for 300 shares. Then, if the stock was opened for trading at 49 3/4, 2,100 shares of customer buy orders would be executed against 1,600 shares of customer sells, with the specialist selling the 500 shares imbalance.

Finally, remember that specialists are expected to open the stock for trading each morning as close as possible to the previous night's close.

TRADING FOR PRESENT AND FUTURE NEEDS

In maintaining their business, specialists are not only supposed to have sufficient inventory to satisfy their present needs, but also their anticipatory need as well. A firm's present inventory is factual and can be proven by position and activity. The second, anticipatory need, is judgmental, and therefore is always subject to scrutiny both by the exchange's regulatory personnel, as well as other members on the trading floor. As specialists are not permitted to freely trade, they cannot use this "anticipatory need" excuse to justify any attempt at free trades. In addition, a specialist transacting business for their own account in anticipation of future needs is not supposed to acquire or sell more than 50% of the stock then offered or bid if said bid or offer is not at the last sale price.

These restrictions on trading are deemed necessary because of the alleged advantages a specialist has in the specialty stock. As the center for trading the particular issue, the specialist is believed to have access to information not afforded the investing public. How much advantage, if any, a specialist has over a technically superior upstairs trading desk can be argued, and is argued every day. Suffice to say, rules are rules.

WHAT A SPECIALIST TRADES

The majority of listed options products that are offered for trading are *equity options* whose underlying security is listed on the New York Stock Exchange (NYSE). As the NYSE is the dominant *equity* exchange, specialists on the *equity* floor have restrictions on their ability to use options to hedge their specialty stock. However, *option* specialists on the American Stock Exchange (Amex), Philadelphia Stock Exchange (Philx), and the NYSE as well as market makers on the Chicago Board of Exchange (CBOE) and the Pacific Stock Exchange (PSE) have no such restrictions on their ability to use the *underlying stock* as a hedge against *their option positions.*

This signifies one of the major differences between the types of specialists mentioned earlier. Due to the cumbersome use of options mandated by Rule 105 of the NYSE, equity specialists shy away from the use of options, whereas option traders use stock freely, and therefore, can assume larger positions with less risk.

Understanding Trading Characteristics

The equity "specialist" must fully understand the trading characteristics of their assigned specialty issue. They must know:

Who are the main participants?

What has been the usual daily volume, of late?

How has the stock performed against the market as a whole, both in relation to volume and the market's value direction?

While the specialists are not supposed to become familiar with the corporate management, they are familiar with research reports, as well as other forms of fundamental research made available to all by such vendor services. As with most traders, news services provided by such vendors as Quotron or Reuters is a must for the equity specialist.

To give an example of how a specialist must remain sensitive to all of these factors, let's assume you are the specialist in Lotus International. Its trading volume is 5,000–7,000 shares a day.

Suddenly, the volume increases to 25,000–30,000 shares a day. What could cause such a jump in volume? First, ask yourself these 10 basic questions:

1. Did the volume on the exchange change in a corresponding manner?

2. Has the increase in volume caused a change in the market price per share either "up or down"?

3. What about other companies in the same industry? Has their trading volume changed?

4. Is there any item in the research reports that could trigger this type of volume change?

5. Especially in today's world, is the company a "takeover" possibility? If so, by whom?

6. Is the common stock involved in a dividend period?

7. Are there options on the stock? If so, has the option volume increased also?

8. Is the stock part of any *basket trading,* either directly or indirectly involved in an *index arbitrage,* or is someone using it as a surrogate for some other issue(s) that may be more expensive? Basket trading is a concept by which securities are positioned in relation to certain indexes and hedge the position against index futures or index options. This trading concept is discussed later. Sometimes portfolio managers buy baskets of stock so that their portfolio will supplement an index. Clients request this approach to investing at times.

9. Are strategies that utilize a combination of the last three items above (6, 7, and 8) being employed?

10. Has there been anything in the news concerning the products that this company manufactures or supplies to other companies?

Remember, a specialist has affirmative and negative obligations that must be fulfilled at all times. Unlike many of the market's participants, in a situation as described above, a specialist cannot move to the sidelines and see what happens. He must try to sort out the cause of the market change and continue to make a fair and orderly market. However, in the event that trading becomes too hectic or too one-sided, the specialist may request a trading halt until normality can be identified and some semblance of order be reestablished to the trading mechanism. In order for a trading halt to be evoked, floor officials or governors must determine that a condition exists that does not provide the ability to maintain a fair and orderly market.

Understanding Price Movements

The movement of price over time is measured by the term *volatility.* The quicker and more violent a stock can move, the higher its volatility and the greater the chance of profit or loss. Therefore, it is important for the specialist to notice any changes in the volatility of their specialty stocks.

Sometimes a company or its product catches the public's fancy; people coming out of other investments "discover" this issue. Given the right doses of the price/earning ratio, positive general news affecting the company's industry, good projected earnings, a change in macroeconomics perception (an economy with increasing interest rates, or the reverse). In any event, regardless of the reason(s), the specialist must be willing to trade every day the market is open and to take down those positions deemed necessary to maintain a fair and orderly market.

HOW A SPECIALIST TRADES

In carrying out their charges with the public, specialists are prohibited from:

1. Competing with a public market order he is holding. This means that at a specific price, the specialist must allow the public order to be executed first without competition.

2. Competing with a limit order he is holding for the public. An executable public limit order must be filled before the specialist can buy/sell for his own account.

3. A specialist must not "stop stock" for his own account. *Stopping stock* is a process by which the price of execution is guaranteed. For example: The quote is 35 1/4–3/4. The size is 80 × 50 (8,000 bid 5,000 offered). A broker enters the crowd with a public customer's order to buy 1,000 shares at the market. By all rights, the order should be filled at 35 3/4. The broker believes a better price can be obtained, so he bids 35 1/2. If someone sells to the broker's bid and fills the order, the broker, acting on his own, has obtained a better price for the client. However, while bidding the 1/2, should the offer of 3/4 be satisfied and the quote becomes 35 1/2–7/8 or 35 1/2–36, the broker, because he acted on his own, would owe the customer the price of 35 3/4. The broker would have to buy 1,000 at 35 7/8 and/or at 36 in his error account and sell it to the client at 35 3/4 (the price the client was entitled).

Stopping Stock

This is where the specialist steps in. With a quote, as in the previous list, 35 1/4–3/4, 80 × 50, the broker enters the crowd with a public market order to buy 1,000 shares at the market. The broker asks the specialist if he would be willing to *stop stock* at 35 3/4. Stop stock relates to the willingness of the specialist to trade from his own trading account, if necessary, to fill the broker's order. If the specialist agrees to this, the broker can then bid, let's say, 36 1/2. If the bid is accepted, the broker notifies the specialist that the "stop is off"; if, however, a transaction takes place at the offer, the specialist will inform the broker that he is "stopped out."

If the specialist is willing to work with the broker:

1. The broker can give the customer better service.

2. The customer has the opportunity to obtain a "better" price.

3. The investing public has the opportunity to participate in a better market as 35 1/2–3/4 is a tighter quote than 35 1/4–3/4. Tighter quotes translate into liquidity.

As explained previously, a specialist can only stop stock for a broker; if the specialist is willing to trade for his own account, he cannot block or hold a portion of the public size against the stop stock request. Therefore, a specialist is not permitted to stop stock for his own account.

Specialists may not elect stop orders unless they are willing to guarantee that the stop order's execution price will be the same as the electing sale. To review, a *stop order* is a memorandum order that becomes a market order when the market reaches its price or better. *Buy stop orders* carry prices above the current market; *sell stop orders* carry prices below the current market. Or in other words, if the word "stop" does not appear on the order, it will be executable.

Suppose the specialist is holding an order to buy 1,000 RAP at 56 1/2 stop. Also on the specialist's "book" are public orders to sell 800 at 56 1/2 and 1,500 at 56 3/4. If it weren't for the requirement that the electing and executing sale must be at the same price, an unscrupulous specialist could buy the 800 shares of public stock at 56 1/2, thereby "triggering" the stop order, then sell the same 800 shares against the stop order at 56 5/8 with the remaining 200 being completed (public versus public at 56 3/4). The rule states that if the specialist elects the stop order when trading for his account, the execution price must be the same as the electing sale. In the above example, had the specialist executed 100 shares at 56 1/2 in his trading account versus the public order, he would owe all 1,000 shares to the stop order at 56 1/2. How does a specialist, therefore, earn money with all these rules (officially known as negative and affirmative obligations) imposed?

The two revenue streams open to the specialist are "floor brokerage" and trading profits. Specialists will charge floor brokerage fees to member firms for executing certain orders. With the electronic order routing and reporting systems which operate between the exchange floor and the brokerage firms, this form of revenue stream has been greatly curtailed.

Therefore, a specialist earns revenue from managing a position. Primary to the specialist's existence is the maintenance of a fair and orderly market by trading for his own account and risk when an imbalance exists. It is, therefore, of major importance for the specialist to know how to react when an imbalance exists or when the market is indicating that the present price is incorrect. Remember, the neutralizer between supply and demand is price. As a stock is perceived to be undervalued, demand will pick up, pushing the price up until an equilibrium between supply and demand is met. If the stock is deemed to be overpriced, supply will increase, pushing the price down until equilibrium is met.

A specialist cannot stand in the way of this natural phenomenon. Not only would this be illegal, as the specialist would be "fixing" or "setting" the market price, but if the trend was strong enough, the specialist would be financially ruined (such as buying into a down trend and selling on an up trend). What specialists do by trading for their own account is to try to provide price continuity which translates into an orderly market.

For example, the current quote is 35 1/4– 3/4, the next highest bid is 35 1/8, the next lowest offer is 35 7/8. As an investor, how would you feel about investing in a stock which had previous sales of 35 1/4, 35 3/4, 35 3/4, 35 1/4, 35 3/4, 35 1/4, 35 7/8, 35 1/8, 35 7/8, and 35 1/8 depending on whether the trade was against the then prevailing bid or offer? Add to the hodgepodge the possibility of some trades occurring in between the bid and offer and you really would have a confusing trading pattern. To you, the use of a market order would be useless since there really isn't a true market. The specialist, given the aforementioned rules and guidelines, is charged with maintaining price continuity and, therefore, on the exchanges that use this system, trades are usually more uniform (such as, 35 1/4, 35 1/4, 35 3/8, 35 3/8, 35 1/4, 35 1/4, 35 3/8, 35 1/2, 35 1/2, and so on).

SUMMARY

The specialists' role is unique. The best description would be that of a quasitrader. What appears to be a franchised business is offset by a series of rules and regulations which result in a rating system being employed by their peers.

Their business depends on their ability to perform in the eyes of their peers. The specialists decide who will be allocated what products and through this process they can make or break a specialist unit.

Through this review process, the exchanges can monitor the performance of the units. Should the performance fall below certain standards, specialists can lose a product or several products. Those products would be reallocated to one or more units.

Chapter 4

Over-the-Counter Equity Traders

Over-the-counter market makers, or traders, make "markets." They select various securities for which they make bids and offers, or *quotes*. These quotes represent the prices at which the market makers or traders are willing to trade. In most marketplaces, more than one market maker will make quotes on any given issue. Each market maker represents a different firm, commonly known as *dealers*. Through their representation of these dealers, the market makers can negotiate the price of various OTC securities, thereby "creating" a market for that issue.

TRADING COMMON STOCK

Common stock issues that qualify under the standards set by the National Market System will be quoted on the National Association of Securities Dealers Automated Quotation Service (NASDAQ). The NASDAQ is an automated, nationally distributed service available to all dealers, traders, and vendors who will disseminate the information to the public. The service is composed of three levels.

Level 1 appears on vendors' screens showing the best bid (highest) and best offer (lowest) of all the dealer quotes combined.

Level 2 appears on the screens located on the traders' desks and informs traders as to who are the market makers in any given issue and what are their current quotes.

Level 3 looks the same as level 2 but is used by the dealers to change their quotes and their size.

Example: The following shows what might appear on the screen for sample issues in levels 2 and 3:

Park Ave Ltd

Market Maker	*Bid-Offer*
Giant Reckor and Crane	$10\frac{1}{8}-10\frac{1}{2}$
Overland and Underwater	$10\ \ -10\frac{1}{4}$
Bedding and Pillows	$10\frac{1}{8}-10\frac{3}{8}$

Level 1 for *Park Ave Ltd* reveals that the quote is "Bid $10\frac{1}{8}$, Offer $10\frac{1}{4}$."

If Giant Reckor and Crane, one of the market makers appearing above, wanted to change its quote, it would enter the system, make the change, and the change would be reflected on all of the appropriate user screens immediately. With the quotes as stated above, it would appear that Giant Reckor and Crane and Beddings and Pillows are trying to acquire stock since they have the higher bids and Overland and Underwater is the most interested in selling, as it has the lowest offer. Should Overland and Underwater sell stock at "$\frac{1}{4}$" and then not want to sell any more, it would raise its offer above the other two dealers.

Another part of the current market that traders should always make themselves aware of is the *size* of the quote. The size represents the amount of shares being bid or offered at the quote. For example, in the above NASDAQ levels 2 and 3 display, Giant Reckor and Crane offered 10 1/8–10 1/2. Overland and Underwater offered 10–10 1/4. Bedding and Pillows offered 10 1/8–10 3/8. What if the size behind each quote was:

Giant Reckor and Crane	10 1/8–10 1/2	1 × 1
Overland and Underwater	10 –10 1/4	5 × 5
Bedding and Pillows	10 1/8–10 3/8	20 × 20

While Giant Reckor and Crane and Bedding and Pillows are both bidding 10 1/8, Giant Reckor and Crane is only willing to buy 100 shares at 10 1/8; whereas Bedding and Pillows will purchase up to 2,000 shares (20). A 1 in the quote equals 100 shares; 20 equals 2,000 shares. On the offer side, while Overland and Underwater is willing to sell stock at 10 1/4 or the best price, Bedding and Pillows has the largest amount offered at 10 3/8 and may very well be making the "best market" for larger quantity-sized orders.

It is for this reason that the OTC market is known as a *negotiated market.* The dealer that gives the best overall price for the order will "fill" the order and there is no obligation to execute orders against dealers who have better bids or offers for lesser quantities. The traders (buyer/seller) negotiate the price of trade.

BECOMING FAMILIAR WITH THE EQUITY MARKET

As with any complex subject, there is more to equity trading than meets the eye, and definitely more to the marketplace than can be covered in a book of this type. Some of the complexities seem strange when first uncovered; but as one's knowledge of the particular trading market grows, the strangeness does wear off.

A good way to familiarize yourself with the workings of the market is to review a level 2 screen of a well-known and actively traded OTC issue. On level 2, the firms making the best quotes are listed first. As the dealers' quotes widen and "fall off" the market, they are listed in a descending order. Here is an example:

Stock—Jilbar

	Bid	Size
Giant Reckor and Crane	36 1/4–36 1/2	3 × 5
Stone, Forrest and Rivers	36 1/8–36 5/8	1 × 1
Overland and Underwater	36 –36 3/4	1 × 1
Bedding and Pillows	36 – 7	1 × 1

Let's assume that Bedding and Pillows is a well-known institutional *block trading* firm and yet it is displaying the worst quote. Block trading is defined by the NYSE as an order involving more than 20,000 shares. It can also include any order that is larger than the marketplace can absorb and therefore requires special handling. The reason is that all of the quotes revealed by all of these dealers are known as *firm quotes* (meaning the prices at which they are willing to trade). Size states the quantity behind the firm quote.

In the above example, Giant Reckor and Crane will purchase up to 300 shares at 36 1/4 or sell up to 500 shares at 36 1/2. Bedding and Pillows, by placing its quote in the system has announced to the world that it is a dealer in Jilbar. However, the firm of Bedding and Pillows is not equipped to handle volumes of transactions. Its core business is based on fewer transactions having larger amounts of shares per trade. In other words, the firm would rather execute one trade for 25,000 shares than 250 trades of 100 shares each.

Therefore, the quote of 36–37 and the size 1 × 1 represents the dealers *firm* commitment. No one with a small quantity order would call them as there are dealers making better markets ahead of them. Those firms are equipped to handle large quantities of orders.

However, suppose a brokerage firm, let's call it Lake, Pond and Poole, had a client that wanted to buy 50,000 shares of Jilbar. Lake, Pond and Poole's trader would eventually speak to Bedding and Pillows' trader who may say "We'll do all 50,000 at 37," or may even say "we'll honor the best offer" which means Bedding and Pillows would sell 50,000 shares at 36 1/2. Even though Bedding and Pillows never offered stock as low as 36 1/2, it can still trade there if it wants to. Remember, it's a negotiated market.

THE ROLE OF THE EQUITY TRADER

When most people think about traders, it is the equity trader that comes to mind. Most people picture traders sitting on a trading desk armed with an array of CRTs (cathode ray tubes, television type tubes) which display various types of data, buying and selling, selling and buying at a frantic pace under unbelievable pressure, screaming into phones, yelling to other traders, and all the while maintaining an inventory position.

While the picture is correct, it applies to most, if not all, of the products which are traded over the counter. Each trader has his own method of trading, and each has his own trigger points. While pressure and the need for split-second decisions permeates the entire trading environment, there are some fundamental differences between trading equity and debt-type products.

Trading Equity Products and the Cost of Carry

Trading firms permit their traders to maintain positions up to certain limits. This "credit or money line" can be composed of 100% firm financing, or can be part firm financing and a small portion contributed by the individual trader. Regardless of the percentage split, a trading firm will usually finance a good portion of the position. In common stocks, banks will usually lend money on 70% of the inventory's current market value. The firm must use its own capital or its capital plus the trader's capital to finance the rest. The lending bank charges interest on the collateralized loan and, therefore, the firm is losing interest opportunity on the capital it has invested in this inventory. Interest expense is omnipresent. This is only part of a trading firm's cost of carrying the position.

Interest and the Cost of Carry. Stocks, unlike bonds, do not pay interest. Trading debt instruments usually involves the receipt, by the firm, of the interest on their positions known as *interest income*. This income which is paid by the debt issuer can offset part or all of the interest expense associated with the position. In the case of the equity trader, even if the stocks are dividend payers, the expense would not be offset because dividends do not accrue, and dividends paid are reflected in the adjustment to the stock price on the *ex-dividend date*. Therefore, the income earned is lost to the market price adjustment. The interest expense borne by the firm on its position plus the usual operating costs must be covered (earned) before the trade can be considered profitable.

The ex-dividend date is the first day a purchaser of the stock is not entitled to receive the dividend. Before the opening of business that day, the marketplace in which the stock trades adjusts the previous night's closing price to reflect the dividend. For example, a stock closes at $90 per share. Its shareholders have been informed that they are to receive 50 cents per share dividend. Before the opening of business the next day, which we will establish as the ex-dividend date, the stock's price will be adjusted to 89 1/2. Therefore, someone buying the stock on the day before the ex-dividend date would be entitled to receive the 50 cents dividend (pay $90 per share, receive 50 cents dividend for a net of 89 1/2 (89.50)), whereas someone buying the stock on the ex-dividend date would pay 89 1/2 and not receive the dividend.

The ex-dividend date is usually four business days before the record date. It is the owners of the stock of the record date who are entitled to receive the dividend. As such, the last date you can purchase the stock the "regular way" and still be entitled to receive the dividend is five business days before the record date. That trade will settle on the record date. If you purchase the stock the next day (the ex-dividend date), it will settle the day after the record date and so, you are not entitled to the dividend.

To clarify this concept, one must understand that interest paid on loans (debt instruments) is an expense to the borrower. Dividends are paid out of current or retained earnings to the owners or shareholders of the company.

To facilitate the settlement of debt transactions, buyers pay sellers accrued interest as part of the transaction. *Accrued interest* is the interest owed by the borrower since the last interest was paid. For example, a bond pays interest every May and November 1. A transaction occurs which has a settlement date of August 16. The buyer owes the seller interest due on the bonds for the period of May 1 through and including August 15, but excluding the settlement date. (May—30 days, June—30 days, July—30 days, August—15 days, for a total of 105 days.) The buyer of the bond, if still the owner on November 1, will receive the full six months interest (May–November) on November 1. The difference between what the buyer paid in accrued interest to the seller on August 16 (a total of 105 days) and what was received on November 1 (a total of 180 days) is the interest owed to the buyer. (August—15 days, September—30 days, October—30 days, for a total of 75 days. Note that 105 + 75 = 180 days.)

Dividends and the Cost of Carry. Dividends, however, are paid by a company to its owners. As such, when it pays the cash dividend, it is reducing its overall value by the dividend amount. Dividends are *not* an expense to a company but are paid from remaining earnings after all expenses, including taxes, are deducted from revenues (income). If a company is worth $10 million and it pays $100,000 in dividends, the company would be worth $9 million. Interest payments, however, are a cost of doing business and their effect is known before the company's worth is computed. Therefore, a company worth $10 million will be worth $10 million after the interest payment.

The "worth" of the company is reflected in its stock price. If a company's common stock is trading at $40 per share, it is trading there because the market believes that that is what the stock is worth. As interest payments do not effect the company's worth, it will not effect its market price. Dividends, which do effect the company's worth will have a corresponding affect on its market price. A company that pays a $1 per share dividend will see its market value reduced by $1 per share on the ex-dividend date.

When a company declares a dividend, it announces three dates: the *declaration date,* the *record date,* and the *payable date.* In the case of the cash dividend, it could be said that on April 1 (the declaration date) the company announced a $1 per share dividend to registered shareholders on the night of April 15 (the record date). Those shareholders will be paid on May 1 (the payable date).

The ex-dividend date is four business days before the record date and represents the first day a purchaser is not entitled to receive the dividend from one company. On the morning of the ex-dividend date, prior to the commencement of trading, the various marketplaces adjust the market value to reflect the dividend. In the above example, should the stock be trading at $90 per share on April 8 and the company has declared its $1 dividend, the market value would be adjusted to $89 before the opening of business on April 9, four business days (six calendar days) before the record date.

THREE TYPES OF EQUITY TRADERS

In the equity market, there are three levels or types of traders, with variations to the word "trader." The trader which this text is addressing is the *dealer* or *market maker* (an individual working for a firm which has committed capital to trade specific security positions). They risk capital in expectation of earning a profit. These traders "run" several different security positions, adjusting the investments in each according to trading decisions.

It must be pointed out that market makers in securities are no different than other vendors or merchants. They maintain inventory positions that they hope are attractive to the investors. The major difference between these business people and those not in the equity industry is that traders will *buy* and *sell* against the public. Most of the vendors that we do business with on a day-to-day basis just sell to us, the buyer.

Another type of trader doesn't risk capital, as described above, but instead trades active issues. This trader buys securities and offers them for sale immediately or sells securities and tries buying them back just as quickly. Each transaction is attempted to be executed at the minimum *spread* (an attempt to earn as much per 100 shares as quickly as possible). Every transaction cannot be profitable, though. The second best transaction would be "getting out" by using equal buying and selling at the same price. The worst case scenario would be "getting out" or unwinding at a loss.

The third type of "trader" works on a trading desk executing orders for the customers of the firm against the market makers. The trader "shops" the client's order among the various market makers. The size of the orders this trader handles determines the risk being taken. Executing 100 shares in a fairly active market is much different than trying to piece together 50,000 shares of an inactive stock.

This is where the trader's skill and ability shows itself. How was the large order handled? Was it completed at the best price possible? Were all sources for the trade examined? The equity trader we will be looking at is a combination of these three elements with emphasis on the first.

TYPES OF SECURITIES TRADED BY EQUITY TRADERS

What security or types of securities will the trader invest in? The trader could, for example, follow the new issue market. Common stocks are usually brought to market through a form of underwriting known as *negotiated underwriting*. Under this form, a syndicate manager (an investment banking firm) leads underwriters (other investment banking firms) through the issuance process. While some new issues will be listed for trading on an exchange, the majority of new issues are first offered for trading in the OTC market.

Trading New Issues

Traders who follow new issues generally follow the workings of certain underwriters. These syndicate or underwriting firms have reputations for bringing certain types and quality of new issues to the market. As the issue is going through the underwriting distribution process, the OTC traders are following the receptivity of the public. Based on the ease of issuance, those deciding to be market makers in these securities will set their "markets" accordingly.

Example: Stone, Forrest and River (SF&R) is syndicate manager on a new issue. Giant Reckor and Crane (GR&C) is an OTC market maker that has been following the distribution of shares by SF&R and the participating underwriting and selling group firms. If the demand for the new issue outstrips the supply, GR&C will open the quote at a premium (above the new issues offering prices). This is known as a *hot issue.* If the issue is satisfying demand, GR&C will set the quote near the offering price. If the supply of the new issue outstrips the demand, it would be SF&R's problem and not GR&C's to adjust the price or take other steps to make the issue attractive.

The offering price is set by the underwriters and the issuer. It appears in the issue's final prospectus, which must be sent to the clients who purchase the stock on the initial offering. The difference between the offering price and the price paid the issuing corporation is known as the *spread.* It is from this spread that the selling firm's brokers will get paid. The underwriters are compensated for their risk, the syndicate manager (SF&R) is reimbursed for expenses involved in the underwriting, and the participating firms, in general, earn revenue. If all goes well, revenue will result. Any and all problems could hurt or risk the revenue possibility.

Stone, Forrest and River receives a phone call from Giant Reckor and Crane to see how the new issue, *Park Ave Ltd*, is working out. (How is it being received?) The issue has an offering price of $10 per share. Based on SF&R's response, GR&C will set its quote. Assume GR&C's first quote and size is 10–$\frac{1}{4}$ 5 × 5. This means that GR&C will purchase up to 500 shares at $10 and sell up to 500 shares at 10 $\frac{1}{4}$. Clients of those firms participating in the underwriting, as well as clients of firms not involved, may want to purchase Park Ave Ltd. Those who were unable to obtain the stock through the initial public offering because the demand outstripped the supply will now come to the marketplace. Giant Reckor and Crane's trader sells stock at 10 $\frac{1}{4}$ to one or more of these clients. At this point, it is important to note that Giant Reckor and Crane is "shorting" the stock. The trader sold stock at 10 $\frac{1}{4}$ which the firm does not own but has established an "open" market price for. The trader is at risk should the price of Park Ave Ltd rise in value and he is unable to buy the stock at 10 $\frac{1}{4}$ or below.

The trader waits a bit, checks to see at what prices other market makers have decided to trade Park Ave Ltd; the trader checks their quotes. Based on their quotes and the fact that GR&C is short, GR&C's trader raises the bid to 10 1/8 trying to buy stock from any client of any firm who may want to accept a quick profit of $12.50 per 100.

Noticing the other market makers' quotes are creeping upward, GR&C's trader does not want to be the only trader offering stock at 10 1/4. The trader notices that the highest bid "away from him" is 10 1/8 and the lowest offer "away" has become 10 3/8. GR&C's trader immediately changes his quote to 10 1/4–1/2 or 10 1/4–5/8. Remember, the trader doesn't want to "short" any more shares of stock, and in this case, the trader is being forced to buy back the stock at the original sale price due to the competition of the other market makers. Let's assume that a trade does take place at 10 1/4 and the GR&C trader closes out the short position even. There is no trading profit and no loss.

In the previous example, many different and independent events were happening at one time:

A new issue came to market.

The offering price was fair in the minds of the market participants.

Several trading firms entered the market to make markets in this issue.

Some traders entered the marketplace ahead of the others; the "others" taking a more cautious approach.

As the traders competed for business, the spread between the quotes narrowed.

The market "price" caused the GR&C trader to buy back the issue at the same price it was sold.

What could have been different?

The new issue could have been considered overpriced. This would have presented a major problem to the underwriting firms and others participating which were selling the issue to *their* clients. If the market did not believe that $10 was a fair price, these firms would have been stuck with the issue, or worse, *their clients* may have unknowingly agreed to take in the new issue at an unfair price, leaving the clients in an unhappy situation which could cause these firms to lose these clients.

If, however, the market perceived the $10 offering price to be cheap, then the market makers would have been setting much higher price quotes and the clients that acquired the stock through the underwriting issue would have an instant profit. But Park Ave Ltd, the company whose stock is being offered, received too little for its shares thereby making the company's directors unhappy which, in turn, could result in the corporation seeking a new investment banker.

Another situation could have been that instead of many market makers participating in the "after market," few or none could have come forth. In this case, there wouldn't be a liquid market and the clients of the firms who have acquired the stock may have difficulty in selling the issue or even trying to determine a "fair" price. One of the most important aspects of our markets is the liquidity that we, as an industry, are so proud of.

The GR&C trader could have purchased the stock at $10\frac{1}{8}$ instead of selling "short" at $10\frac{1}{4}$. With this purchase, GR&C could have held some, all, or none of the shares in resetting the stock quote. If the trader expected:

A substantial increase in market value, based on the competing market makers' action, the trader would hold the issue until the "frenzy" calmed down and then offer the shares in the marketplace.

Normal pricing action by the market would have the trader going in and out of positions, trying to earn a profit by buying the issue at a lower price than he is selling it at.

But what if $10\frac{1}{8}$ was the highest price paid? The GR&C trader owns the stock at the "high." In all probability, the trader will "dump" the stock and accept the loss.

In these three scenarios all actions were based on short-term views. A trader's long-term opinion about a stock or a situation could drastically change any of the decision-making processes described.

For example, suppose the new issue was priced fairly at $10 per share, but on the day the syndicate broke, the market, in general, was "soft" and therefore prices on most issues were "off" slightly. The trader could buy the issue in the soft market and wait for the market to "firm up" or simply trade it. Both strategies have their own inherent risks. For example, what if the stock is trading at a strong price in a soft market and when the market firms up the stock remains at its price, or worse, the stock loses its momentum and loses value as the market firms up. The terms *firm, soft, strong,* and *weak* can be misleading as they are nothing more than a professional interpretation of an existing condition.

A *firm market* generally means prices are holding, even though there is some selling pressure. A *soft market* generally means prices are off (down) slightly and very susceptible to selling pressure. A *strong market* refers to demand for issues outstripping supply and prices, in general, are rising. A *weak market* means prices are generally falling. These descriptions must be taken into consideration in terms of what is happening outside the market news. On a macro level, a given market condition can be defined as firm or soft in light of good or bad news. For example, the fact that prices are "off" (down) slightly, could be considered a soft market in the face of good or no news. It could be considered a strong market in view of poor news. We have all heard commentators say "the market remained firm in light of . . . ."

Trading Industry Related Issues

Besides trading new issues, OTC equity traders select their inventory on other criteria such as industry or industry related groupings. By knowing corporate issues in certain segments of the marketplace, traders take positions and trade from them.

Dunbar Associates is an OTC firm that has traders who are specialized by industry group. One trader specializes in automotive issues, another in computer software (Silicon Valley) type issues, and so on.

The automotive specialist follows issues of those corporations that supply automotive products to manufacturers and retail sales outlets. As most major manufacturers have their common stocks listed for trading on the equity exchanges, the OTC traders generally choose not to be involved with these, but specialize in issues which are traded in the OTC market.

The computer industry, especially certain hardware manufacturers and software suppliers, usually retains common stock in an OTC status. This segment of the industry has provided one of the most dynamic growth areas for trading issues. Hundreds, if not thousands, of these computer-based companies have brought their stocks to market. Some have been highly successful, others well. . . . The traders who specialize in this field *must* stay on top of the market, as to be caught "asleep at the switch" may result in severe financial embarrassment. Which company has announced what product, how good it is, what will it replace, who is affected by it, and so on are all questions whose answers play a vital part in the market maker's decision process as to how to manage his/her inventory.

For example, what would you do if these facts "hit" your trading desk at once? Rometecks is a major manufacturer of microprocessors. Their Model 444 has been out for some time and has gained a reputation for reliability. Venezel has played second place to Rometecks in this segment of the industry but has just introduced Model J47, which is twice as fast and has four times the memory capacity of Rometecks' Model 444. Rometecks' new model is due to be on the market in six to nine months, but the actual specifications are unknown. A third company, Frenzianics, has been pushing a microprocessor that it claims makes all others obsolete. Frenzianics is a new company whose manufacturing capability is questionable. However, Rometecks and several other companies have the financial wherewith-all to buy out Frenzianics, although no talks between the companies are known to exist.

As a trader, would you buy Rometecks and hold it in position? What about Venezel; will its Model J47 push the company ahead of Rometecks in sales, and can it sustain its new found lead? Could this firm be the "winner"? Finally, what about Frenzianics? Is this the giant of the future? If you think this is farfetched, just follow articles in the newspaper for a while. How old do you think real companies such as Intel, Apple, and Compaq really are?

The tracking by industry or industry group also includes companies that are controlled by known, needed, or benchmarked products such as gold, chemicals (related to the oil industry), and petroleum. Factors affecting these critical commodities or products affect the corporations that operate in these areas. Traders that operate in the stocks must monitor different forms of information. Gold prices are established by many forces other than industry. In the case of oil, the name OPEC (Organization of Petroleum Exporting Countries) is known by all. As the value of these basic commodities change, entire industries are affected as are their products and their buying public.

Trading "Hot" Stocks

Still other traders may look for "hot" stocks. They trade whatever appears to be exciting under the premise "where there is smoke, there is fire." If the volume of trading in a given issue increases markedly, the reason is not of importance to these traders. What is important is the volume and direction the price of the issue is taking. These traders usually do not maintain large overnight positions due to unexpected changes in market conditions. A stock trading strong and "hot" today may be "cold" tomorrow. Therefore, these traders buy and sell quickly, trying to make profits from the spread. If they maintain a position, it is usually small and they are maintaining the position augmenting the trend. As soon as the trend appears to weaken, the traders will get out of the position.

Traders do the reverse when they follow a downward trend. They try to maintain a short position, buying the shares in at prices lower than what they were sold. In other words, going short, covering at a lower price, then selling more shares short, and so on. The traders follow the trend down until it appears to "bottom out." Once the activity in a particular issue quiets down, the traders go on to trade different securities.

Trading Issues in Blocks

The final type of OTC trader to be discussed is the *block trader*. These individuals work to put shares of a given stock together to satisfy the needs of their clients.

For example, the Satin Trust has accumulated 100,000 shares of Emily Frocks over a period of time. The trust has maintained the position for some time and now wants to sell the issue. The market cannot absorb a quantity this size in a reasonable fashion. Satin Trust is also concerned about the price they will receive. As a block of this size could depress the price (meaning the trust would not receive full value), a block trader will enter the picture and try to put buyers together that will total the 100,000 shares.

The block trader starts by contacting other institutions that have either previously indicated an interest in this type of issue or may own shares of Emily Frocks at the present time. The trader may contact a research firm to determine if there has been favorable reports issued recently. If, in fact, there has been, the trader will follow up with the listed users of this research to see if interest still exists in acquiring the stock.

A block trader will even contact a block trader at another firm in search of security interest. If the trader places Satin Trust's stock at a fair price, Satin Trust is happy, the clients on the other side of the trade are happy, and the block trader has, in fact, enhanced his reputation.

There are times that a block trader may have to "take down" some of the position and hold it overnight. Sometimes, they must maintain the position for a longer period of time. This is done to accommodate a good client while the security is in position. The block trader is at market risk and will try to work out the position by competing with other market makers.

CORPORATE TRADER INSTINET

Instinet is an "electronic" trading system. It offers traders the ability to see the primary market makers' quotes and indications of interest in trading "blocks" while monitoring the transactions in other securities all at one time, and all on the same screen (see Figure 4.1).

The primary market makers, which are located on the upper left-hand side of the screen represent levels 2 and 3 of the NASDAQ. The dealers whose quotes are displayed have level 3

Figure 4.1. *Sample Instinet Quote.*

11:52 AAPL. SELL 5,000 39.6 ... DEC&N 103.2/103.6 20×20
11:52 FGRP. SELL 10,000 59.1 ... NSM&MADF 10.7/11.2 10×15
11:52 UK. BUY 4,300 23.1 ... DEC&C 103.2/104 5×10
11:52 MAXI & DEAN 3.6/3.7 1.1 ... XON . BUY 10,000 38.7 ... MCIC&Q 2,000 – 9.1
11:51 IBM & N 113.1 35×100 ... GM&B 5,000 – 58.6 ... INGR . SELL 2,000 20.0

RAR REID & WRIGHT — Present-9 — Last&T 3,000 — 28.0+ — Up 0.11 — V 915,000

Interests-20

Age		Bid	Ask	Size	Buy O&N 27.7		28.0+ H&N 28.3		Up 0.11 L&N 27.6	Sell		
3	N	28.0′	28.2′	300×20	28.1	25,000			28.2	35,000	T	11:22
8	B	28.0′	28.2′	100×20	28.0	15,000			28.1	15,000	T	11:15
1	M	28.0′	28.2′	20×20	28.1	35,000	A	11:22	28.1	20,000	A	10:00
3	X	28.0′	28.2′	1×1	27.7	5,000	T	9:45	27.7	18,000	X	9:37
3	P	28.0′	28.4′	20×21	27.7	13,000	T	10:00	27.6	10,000		
9	C	27.7	28.3	5×5	27.4	20,000	T	11/31	27.5	55,000	A	11/31
25	MADF	27.6	28.3	10×20	27.5	9,000	T	11/31	27.6	25,000	T	11/27
35	TRIM	27.6	28.4	10×10	27.6	45,000	A	11/27	27.4	5,000	T	11/25

11:52 DJI 1,890.85 –11.78 V&N 86.2m (92.4) TIC –34 (c) INSTINET

Source: Adapted from Instinet

access, giving them the ability to change their quotes. Anyone else accessing this screen has level 2 access, which only displays a list of the primary dealers.

A salient feature of the Instinet System is the Instinet Book. This book gives subscribers the ability to advertise a block position at a net price for a given period of time. For example, an equity trader can offer 225,000 shares of Reid & Wright at 22 $\frac{1}{2}$ until 11:30 A.M. At 11:30 A.M., the offer will automatically be canceled. Should someone want to trade, he can enter the interest into the system and a trade would occur. If, however, the buyer wanted to counterbid, the trader would enter the bid giving the trading constraints (e.g., Buy = 225,000 Reid & Wright @ 22 $\frac{1}{4}$ good until 11:00 A.M.). If the trader making the offer decided to accept the bid, a trade would take place at 22 $\frac{1}{4}$. The trader would cancel the offer at 22 $\frac{1}{2}$. However, the trader could counteroffer 22 $\frac{3}{8}$ and the buyer could then counter bid at 22 $\frac{5}{16}$, and so on.

The Instinet "pad" also records accumulated shares against certain orders. This tells the trader watching the screen how much interest there is in a particular issue at a given price. Instinet also provides its subscribers with a stock monitor. Based on parameters set by the user, the system will alert the user when the stock activity that interests him reaches these set parameters.

As you review the Instinet screen, notice how much data is available at a glance. Based on that data, a trader can enter the system and negotiate a price with another trader which will eventually lead to an execution. Instinet is valuable as a monitor and a working tool for any corporate trader.

SUMMARY

We have explored the world of the OTC equity trader. This position is the one most people think of when they think of the trader; the high-powered, high-pressured individual that wheels and deals the world's wealth away; the steel-boned individual that we have seen in movies, on TV, and so forth and have grown to love (or hate).

In reality, this individual requires a constant flow of news and statistics in order to operate. Armed with various data streams, the individual interprets the data and makes market action decisions. The decisions blend into strategies and these strategies develop into that individual's trading habits.

Chapter 5

Debt Traders

The largest dollar portion of our marketplace is devoted to *debt trading*. A *debt instrument* is a document specifying the terms and conditions of any loan between a lender and a borrower. Before we get into the differences between debt instruments and the ways that they are traded, it is important to understand key factors affecting the trading of those instruments.

FACTORS INFLUENCING TRADES OF DEBT INSTRUMENTS

Interest Rates

Interest rates fluctuate. That's a fact of life! They rise, they fall. The cost of money is one of the most important factors in managing a business, governmental agencies, or our private lives. It could be the difference between profit and loss or between loss and bankruptcy.

The vast majority of the debt instruments that we trade are *fixed income instruments*. This means that the rate of interest paid by the issuer is set at the time of issuance. The rate, or percentage, reflects the current (going) market conditions at the time of issuance. As interest rates change, the instrument's value must be adjusted. As the rate of interest is fixed, the *price* or *value* of the instrument must, therefore, change.

Example: Let's assume that in the year 1980 it would cost the Varga Corporation 8% to borrow long-term money in the marketplace. At that time, the public was willing to give $1,000 for $1,000 of Varga's debt. Ten years later, in 1990, interest rates have risen to the point where if Varga Corporation wanted to borrow long-term money, it would cost 9%. Varga, a good growth company, decides to issue the debt and receives one dollar for every dollar of debt, paying 9% interest annually. If both bonds were equal to each other in all other aspects besides their interest rate, which bond would you be willing to purchase in 1990?

1,000 VAR 8% FA 2009 @ $1,000

or

1,000 VAR 9% FA 2009 @ $1,000

Obviously, you would choose the 9% bond. To make the 8% bond attractive, the purchase price would have to be lowered to the point where the rate of return on *your* investment would be the same or similar.

The point of the above example is that as interest rates rise, bond (debt) prices fall and, therefore, yields rise. Conversely, as interest rates fall, bond prices rise and yields fall.

Time

Another factor affecting the price or value of a debt instrument is the period of time that the debt is to remain outstanding.

Usually, the longer the term, the higher the interest rate of return. This is due to the length of time the lender's money is exposed to market risk. Translation: "What if I need my money back," asks the lender. "How long do I have to wait and for how long am I exposed to market value changes?" A debt instrument of 3 months duration is different from a debt instrument with 3 years duration, both of which are different from a debt instrument with 30 years duration. People's financial conditions change over time as does the economy, and the question should be "How long can I afford to have my finances exposed to market risk?"

One's perception of the marketplace as a whole changes from time to time. Economic climate, inflation, recession, and so on all play a key role in the setting of interest rates. Collectively, this perception is known as the *market price* of the instrument. The previous paragraph contained the phrase "*Usually* the longer the term, the higher the rate of return." The word *usually* is used because there are conditions that can cause this not to happen. Suppose the perception of the marketplace was that interest rates were going to fall. Investors would sell their short-term instruments in order to buy longer term debt so as to lock in the current higher rate. The effect on the market price would be that the near-term market value would fall (and rates of return would rise) because of the selling pressure. Long-term rates would rise (and rates of return would fall) because of the buying pressure. This could evolve to the point that the short-term market would give a higher rate of return than the long-term market.

Financial Strength of Issuer

The final factor to be discussed which has an effect on interest rates of return, is the financial strength of the issuer. A financially strong and well-known issuer has a better reputation within the marketplace. This makes it easier for such an entity to borrow money. At the time of issuance, the vehicle used to neutralize these differences between issuers is the *coupon* or interest rate affixed to the instrument. An issuer who has a good reputation and who is financially strong will qualify with a lower interest rate.

U.S. Treasury debt instruments are of the highest possible quality because they are backed by the full faith and credit of the

U.S. government. Due to this fact, there is an ongoing high demand for these instruments. Therefore, the government pays the lowest percent of interest, or to say it in other terms, if a group of bonds from different issuers was brought to market at the same time, U.S. Treasury instruments would carry the lowest coupon rate. (Note that interest rates would be adjusted for income tax considerations.)

RATING THE ISSUES

There are services that rate the creditworthiness of debt instrument issuers. Two of the best known entities in this field are *Moody's* and *Standard & Poor's*. These organizations "rate" the issuer and the issue against their established criteria and publish their evaluation. For example, the strongest issuers will be AAA rated. As this top grade company issues "layers" of debt instruments (each debt is junior to the preceding debt), the ratings of the junior debt may not be AAA rated. In addition, based on the creditworthiness of the collateral against which the loan is being taken, one debt instrument may have a different rating from another instrument of the same issuer. Moody's and Standard & Poor's have slightly different ratings systems, but the new trader will soon get the hang of each system.

Again, the higher the rating the lower the yield or, at the time of issuance, the lower the coupon or interest rate.

Example: Three different companies are bringing 30-year bonds to the market. One is AAA rated, one AA rated, and one is BBB rated.

Rating	Company	Debt Instrument		Price
AAA	McLaughlin Liquid Fuel Co.	MLF	8% FA–2008	Par
AA	Surfside Sand Corp.	SSC	8 3/8% FA–2008	Par
BBB	Livingston Compass Corp.	LCC	9% FA–2008	Par

In the above example, the company rated BBB is paying 1 percentage point of interest more than the AAA-rated company has to pay in order to raise their needed money.

If the loan was for $50 million, it would cost the BBB-rated company $500,000 per year or $15 million over the life of the bond to borrow the same amount of dollars as the AAA-rated company.

The ratings used by Moody's and Standard & Poor's can be viewed in similar fashion to school grades. Assume a school has the following standards:

90–100 = A

80–89 = B

70–79 = C

and so on

Three individuals take a final exam and receive the grades of 100%, 91%, and 88%, respectively. By the school's standard, the students with a grade of 100% and a grade of 91% would receive the grade of A, whereas the third student would receive a grade of B. On further inspection, the grade of 91 is closer to the grade of 88 than it is to the grade of 100. Therefore, to give the 100 and the 91 percent students the same grade may be considered unfair. To put the concept into bond terms, would *you* be willing to pay the same price for something that is only 91% "perfect" as you would pay for something that is 100% "perfect"? The answer should be *no*! Therefore, the marketplace adjusts for these aberrations and the degree of imperfection is reflected in the bond price. In other words, all bonds rated the same do not trade at the same price. Using the above example, the price of the bond that just qualified as "grade A" will be trading at a value closer to the "grade B" bond than it would be the 100% grade A Bond.

YIELDS

There is no such place as the Gold-lined Road and no such place as Easy Street, Utopia. The markets containing interest sensitive issues, such as fixed income securities, are highly competitive. The different products have very strong interrelationships. Therefore, debt instruments are usually fairly priced in relationship to the other instruments.

The most important principle in dealing with these instruments is the *rate of return* or *yield.* An investor may ask himself, "What sum or percentage is being earned on my investment?" "Is it worth the return I am receiving?" "What is the yield?" When discussing yields, it is most important to understand which instrument is being discussed and in what context the terms are being used.

Current Yield

Current yield is the market value divided into annual interest payments.

For example, bond, $1,000 RAP 8% FA–2018, is trading at 90 (the price of 90 refers to 90% of the face amount of the loan). From the bond description, we can ascertain that the bond will pay $80 per year (8% of its face $1,000). Payments will be made in February and August (FA) and it matures in the year 2018. The current yield is:

$$\$80 \div 900 = 8.88\%.$$

Note that the bond's current yield is higher than its coupon rate. This relationship is very important in understanding trading.

As another example, if bond, $1,000 PIP 10% MS–2008, is trading at 110½ ($1,105), from the bond description we can ascertain that the bond pays 10% on its face ($1,000), pays twice a year March and September (MS) and matures in the year 2008. The current yield will be computed:

$$\$100 \div 1,105 = 9.05 \text{ (approximately)}.$$

Again, note the relationship between the bond's current yield and its coupon rate. In the case where the price was lower than par, or 100%, the yield was higher than the coupon rate. When the price was higher than par, the yield was lower than the coupon rate.

Yield to Maturity

Another yield calculation of major importance is the *yield to maturity rate*. The calculation for yield to maturity includes the computation for current yield, plus it accounts for the difference between purchase or current price and par. This difference is amortized (below par) or depleted (above par) over the remaining life of the bond.

For example the yield to maturity for a bond quoted as $1,000 ZAP 12% FA–(20 years remaining) at 110 would be:

$1,100 Current value
$1,000 Value at maturity
$ 100 Loss over 20 years

$100 ÷ 20 = $5 loss per year (depletion)

This would indicate $120 interest paid per $1,000 of the face amount. The formula for this interest is:

$$\frac{\text{Interest} + \text{Amortized} - \text{Depleted value}}{\left(\dfrac{\text{Current market value} + \text{Value at maturity}}{2}\right)}$$

$$\frac{\$120 - \$5}{\left(\dfrac{\$1,100 + \$1,000}{2}\right)} = \frac{\$115}{\$1,050} = .1095$$

$$= 10.95\%$$

Another example of yield to maturity for a bond quoted as $1,000 RAM 8% AO–(30 years remaining) at 70 would be:

$1,000 Value at maturity
$ 700 Current market value
$ 300 Profit at the end of 30 years

$300 ÷ 30 years = $10

$$\frac{\$80 + \$10}{\left(\dfrac{\$700 + \$1,000}{2}\right)} = \frac{\$90}{\$850} = .10588$$

$$= 10.59\%$$

Again, notice in the above two examples the relationship between the market price versus the coupon rate and the resulting yield to maturity. Again, if the market value is higher than par, the yield is lower than the coupon rate. When the market value is lower than par, the yield is higher than the coupon rate.

Some of the instruments we trade contain a *call feature*. This permits the issuer to retire the issue when it is advantageous for the issuer to do so. The call feature usually carries a price at which the issuer can exercise this feature. Let's assume that a 1,000 RAP 10% MS (30 years) at par, but callable in 10 years at 105. The yield to maturity is 10% and would be calculated as follows:

$$\frac{\$100 \pm 0}{\left(\dfrac{\$1,000 + \$1,000}{2}\right)} = \frac{\$100}{\$1,000} = .10$$

$$= 10\%$$

The price to call is

$$
\begin{array}{ll}
\$1,050 & \text{Call price} \\
\underline{\$1,000} & \text{Current market price} \\
\$\ \ 50 & \text{Profit}
\end{array}
$$

$$50 - 10 \text{ years} = \$5.00$$

$$\frac{\$100 + \$5}{\left(\dfrac{\$1,050 + \$1,000}{2}\right)} = \frac{\$105}{\$1,025} = 1,024$$

$$= 10.24\%$$

If the bonds are called in 10 years, the owner will have a yield of 10.24%, but if the issuer does not call the bonds but retires the bonds at maturity, the yield would be 10% based on the purchase price of par. In dealing with this instrument, the difference between the two can lead to either a great decision or a "bummer." If the bonds are called in between the two dates, the yield to maturity would be based on the "call price" in effect at that time.

Certain instruments do not mature but deplete over time. This method of retirement is found in certain *mortgage-backed securities*. These issues are securitized pools of mortgages or securities backed by pools of mortgages issued by mortgage bankers, commercial banks, savings banks, and other institutions. As the mortgagees pay down their debt, the payments are passed along to the security holder. In this fashion, the amount of debt outstanding is constantly decreasing until it is depleted.

Yields to Average Life

To compute yield to maturity on mortgage-backed securities would be worthless as the majority of instruments or all of the debt will be retired before maturity. To replace yield to maturity, the users of this instrument employ a concept known as *average life*. For example, a 25-year GNMA modified pass-through (instruments of the Government National Mortgage Association (GNMA)) has an "average life" of 15 years. Yields are computed on yields to average life. If the instruments deplete before the 15 years, the length outstanding has been overstated. If, however, the instruments remain outstanding for more than 15 years, the calculation would be understated.

Some debt traders concentrate on short-term instruments and trade either/or *commercial paper, bankers' acceptances,* or *certificates of deposit.* Collectively, these instruments are part of the money market instrument field. Issued for a short period of time, these instruments trade in relationship to U.S. Treasury Bills, which are the short-term instruments of the federal government. We will go into more detail concerning the trading of mortgage-backed securities in Chapter 9.

SUMMARY

Welcome to the world of the debt instrument. As introduced in this chapter, it is a multifaceted segment of our industry which has many interrelationships between products. The idiosyncrasies of the instruments themselves lead to an interesting world of trading. The products' relationships to one another, as well as fixed income and money market instruments' relationships to the economy, the action of "Fed," the world at large, and many other stimuli make these products highly tradable as well as highly desirable.

Chapter 6

Corporate Bond Traders

One of the major advantages of the corporate form of business is its ability to raise capital, not only through stock issuance (ownership), but through the issuance of debt instruments as well. The debt may take the form of short-term commercial loans and commercial paper, intermediate-term notes, or long-term bonds. The instrument that will be focused on here is the long-term debt known as *corporate bonds*.

UNDERSTANDING CORPORATE DEBT

What is corporate debt? What security is behind it? Municipals and U.S. Treasuries are generally secured by the issuer's ability to tax or charge fees. But what about corporations which have stockholders who are owners? What supports their debt? How can corporations issue debt?

Four Types of Corporate Debt Instruments

A well-known and safe corporation could issue debt backed by nothing but its "good name." These instruments are known as *debentures.* A debenture is an unsecured debt offering by a corporation, promising only the general assets of the corporation as protection for creditors. Railroads, airlines, and trucking companies issue debt against their rolling stock. These instruments are known as *equipment trusts.* Equipment trust bonds are bonds collateralized by the machinery and/or equipment of the issuing corporation.

Newer or less well-known companies issue debt against securities from other issuers. These are known as *collateral trusts.* A collateral trust bond is a bond issue that is protected by a portfolio of securities held in trust by a commercial bank. A newer company may have obtained these securities from pledges of wealthy stockholders or through contributions of a major shareholder for the purpose of issuing the particular debt.

A fourth type of debt is *mortgage bonds* issued against plants and office buildings owned by the corporation. A mortgage bond is a bond whose payments are secured by a set of mortgages. The mortgage bonds may be open-ended or close-ended. *Open-ended* means that the issuer can issue additional debt which is equal to initial debt. *Close-ended* means that any subsequent issue is junior to the issue being reviewed.

PRICE DISCOVERY CRITERIA OF CORPORATE DEBT

Callability and Duration

Corporate debt may be *callable,* which means that the issuer has the right to retire the debt or "call in" the issue before maturity if they want to. The call feature is, first of all, evoked when it is most disadvantageous to the investor and is called at a price described in the bond's indenture. The *indenture* or *deed of trust* appears on the bond certificate and describes the terms of the debt. The terms of the debt are also reproduced in many of the industry's digests, which are accessible to participants. (Some versions can be found in public libraries for those who may want to do their own research.)

Corporate bond traders rely on this information and much more, as will become evident as you read on, in determining which bonds to buy and sell, sell and buy, buy and hold, or simply stay away from.

Issuing Criteria and Interest Rates/Coupon Rates

By definition, bonds can be issued for periods of from 10 to 30 years in length. (Notes are usually issued from 1 to 10 years.) A corporation would set the time duration by reviewing the collateral supporting the debt and the market perception of interest rates over time. Generally, the longer the investment is exposed to market risk, the greater will be the demand for compensation. This is known as the *interest rate of return.*

While the amount of interest that must be paid varies over time, the degree of differences between the maturity periods also changes. It is normal for longer-term instruments to carry higher coupon rates than the equivalent shorter-term instrument issued at the same time.

However, the amount of the difference changes as the marketplace's perception of interest rates changes; and, in fact, could even evolve to a point where "near-term" rates are higher than long-term rates. Many studies have been performed and numerous textbooks have been written on the effect of interest rates, the perception thereof, and its relationship to time. It is an interesting and integral part of our business and should be understood by anyone seeking to enter the fixed income security business.

As corporate bonds and notes are part of the fixed income security segment of our marketplace, the value of the instruments fluctuates as interest rates change. As interest rates rise, bond prices fall causing yields to rise. Conversely, as interest rates fall, bond prices rise and yields fall. The rate or amount of interest paid by these instruments is *fixed* or *set* at the time of issuance. Therefore, in order to keep them tradable in the marketplace, something must "give" to accommodate the changing world.

For example, in 19xx the Sugar Coat Company issued a 30-year bond and received $1,000 for every $1,000 of debt. The then going interest rate for a company like Sugar (symbol SGR) was 12%. Over the next 10 years, interest rates have fallen and in 19xx, the company comes to the market to issue a 20-year bond. To receive $1,000 for every $1,000 of debt, the company must pay 9%. If both bonds were trading at *par* ($1,000 for each $1,000 of debt), which would *you* purchase?

> Bond 1 is quoted $1,000 SGR   12% of 200X @ par.
>
> Bond 2 is quoted $1,000 SGR   9% of 200X @ par.

Bond 1 is paying $120 per $1,000; bond 2 is paying $90 per $1,000. As both bonds are issued by the same corporation and are assumed, in this example, to be financially equal, which bond would you acquire for $1,000? Obviously, the 12% bond as you would be receiving $120 interest per year for your $1,000 investment versus $90. The preference or bias toward the 12% bond would be reflected in the bond's price. Either the 12% would increase in market value or the 9% would decrease, or both. The determining factor is where the bonds stand in relationship to other bonds in the marketplace at a given point in time and where interest rates are at that given point in time.

The relationship that exists between the coupon rate of the bond and its price produces yields. This answers the question "What am I getting back on my investment?" As interest rates rise, bond prices fall and yields rise. As interest rates fall, bond prices rise and yields fall.

Example: The Stepfan Corporation brings 20-year bonds to the market. At the time of issue, based on where the Stepfan Corporation fits into the hierarchy of debt instruments, the company's debt has to carry a coupon rate of 9% to successfully compete with other instruments and have investors willing to pay $1,000 for each $1,000 of debt. With the newly issued bond carrying a

9% coupon and trading at par, both the current yield and the yield to maturity are at 9%.

The *current yield* is the market value divided into amount of interest or:

$$\$1,000 \div \$90.00 = .09 = 9\%.$$

The *yield to maturity* is the annual interest payment plus annualized amortized discount or minus the annualized depleted amount over the average value (current market value + value at maturity divided by 2) or:

$$\frac{\$90 \pm 0}{\left(\dfrac{\$1,000 + \$1,000}{2}\right)} = \frac{\$90}{\$1,000} = .09 = 9\%$$

Let's assume interest rates were to rise to the point where Stepfan's outstanding bonds could no longer be sold or traded at 9% yield. For Stepfan to remain tradable, it would have to yield closer to 10%. As the coupon rate on the bond is fixed at 9%, the price would have to "give." Let's assume a price of 90 (which means 90% of face amount of debt or, in the case of a $1,000 face amount of loan, $900).

With the market price per $1,000 of principal debt worth $900, the bonds would continue to pay 9% interest on the face or principal amount of debt, or $90 per $1,000. At a market price of $900, a new investor would be receiving $90 interest on an investment of $900. This would be calculated as:

$$\text{Current yield} = \$900 \div \$90 = 10\%.$$

Therefore, the yield to maturity would be calculated as follows:

Value at maturity	$1,000
Less market value	$ 900
Gain	$ 100

$100 gain divided by years life remaining (in this case 20 years)

$$\$100 \div 20 = \$5$$

Average value minus current market value plus value at
maturity divided by 2

$$\frac{\$900 + \$1,000}{2} = \$950$$

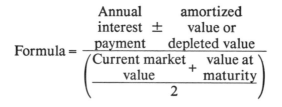

$$\text{Formula} = \frac{\begin{array}{c}\text{Annual} \quad\;\; \text{amortized}\\ \text{interest} \;\pm\;\; \text{value or}\\ \text{payment} \quad \text{depleted value}\end{array}}{\left(\dfrac{\text{Current market} \; + \; \text{value at}}{\text{value} \qquad\quad \text{maturity}}\right)}$$

$$\frac{\$90 + \$5}{\left(\dfrac{\$900 + \$1,000}{2}\right)} = \frac{\$95}{\$950} = 10\%*$$

Financial Strength of Issuer

We have viewed two criteria in the price discovery procedures used by traders to determine the profitability of corporated
debt instruments. One was duration and the other was the instrument's coupon rate. A third criteria is the safety or financial
strength of the issuer. The better capitalized the issuer, the lower
the interest rate or yield; or, conversely, the higher the risk, the
higher the coupon rate or yield.

For example, the following three instruments are trading at
par ($1,000 for $1,000 of debt). How much more interest would
you be expecting to receive in order to entice you to buy the
second issue instead of the first; or the third issue instead of
the other two? Only the coupon rate of the first debt instrument
will be shown. Using our previous calculations, which one is the
better issue?

1. U.S. Treasury Bond - 7% Coupon Maturing July 1, 2019
Trading @ Par

* In this case, current yield and yield to maturity compute to the same
yield. This is not always true.

2. Major, financially sound Corporation's Bond _____ Coupon Maturing July 1, 2019 Trading @ Par

3. Unheard of, financially weak Corporation's Bond_____ Coupon Maturing July 1, 2019 Trading @ Par

In order for all three instruments to be trading at par, and as all three mature on July 1, 2019, the time left to maturity is the same, their respective coupon rates must be different. In the above example, assuming the bonds were issued in the same period, the higher the risk, the higher the coupon. The question is, and one that separates a good trader from the rest, is how much greater? Should the major corporate bond carry a coupon of 7 3/4%, or maybe 8%, or 8 1/4%? The actual coupon rate carried by the bond will determine its market price. A good trader will assess whether the bond is undervalued (should be bought) or overvalued (should be sold). Once the decision is made, market action is taken and the trader waits for the market value to adjust. How long should you wait? When do you admit to an error in judgment? These are the marks of a good trader.

In setting these rates, traders try to ascertain as much information as possible about the particular issue or issues. Generally this information is gathered over time as the trader follows certain products or events. A trader cannot stop during the day, leave the trading desk, and go to a research library. The information is gathered, stored, and updated by such sources as newspapers and newsservices. It is this last data source which separates the great trader from the rest.

Not all news affecting the price of an issue is a direct "hit" such as "Standard & Poor's has lowered the rating on Gaff and Smyte Ltd." It could be the effects of a military contract going or not going to a major contractor which in turn hires Gaff & Smyte as a subcontractor, or a news report that affects the company/industry, or even a series of events leading to an adjustment of the price discovery. For example, the federal government is going to increase expenditures in such and such which could cause interest rates to rise, but the impact of the expenditure on this particular company will be very beneficial, strengthening its balance sheet and thereby making the issue(s) more attractive, raising its market price and lowering its yield.

Corporate bond and note traders must therefore be cognizant of interest rates and events that could affect them, but also of companies and those events that could affect the financial fibers of the company.

Traders who are familiar with certain issues and/or issuers will track the way debt instruments trade and will take action when a discrepancy occurs in this pattern. For example, bonds of the Costanza Smithing Company and Irwin International usually trade a half a point (known as 50 basis points) apart. During the course of a trading day, the Costanza bonds rise to a point (100 basis points) over the Irwin instrument. As there is no apparent reason besides trading activity for this break in continuity, a trader would sell (short) the Costanza bond and buy the Irwin debt. If all of the trader's assumptions are correct, the two instruments should return to the $1/2$ point difference, at which time the trader will "buy" the Costanza bonds and sell the Irwin bonds making a $1/2$-point profit. It is also possible that something is awry at one of the corporations and this price difference could widen. The instruments would never return to their previous "spread" which will result in a loss to the trader.

It is important to note, in the above example, that it doesn't matter if bond prices in general rise or fall; what is important is that the price difference between the two instruments return to their usual relationship.

THE CONVERSION FEATURE OF CORPORATE DEBT

Corporations issue the only debt which could contain a feature that permits conversion into another security, usually common stock. This conversion feature is offered to attract investors to acquire the issue while affording the issuer the ability to get out of the debt at a later date.

Example: $1,000 Regal Corporation 8% FA 2018 @ par is convertible into 25 shares of Regal common stock at $40 a share.

What this example is stating is that Regal Corporation has incurred a $1,000 debt on which it will pay 8% interest ($80 per year) or $40 will be paid on February 1; the other $40 paid on August 1, and the bond will mature in the year 2018. As it is trading at par, the buyer will pay $1,000 for the instrument.

As the instrument is at par, the conversion feature allows the buyer to exchange the $1,000 bond for 25 shares of stock. If the stock is trading at $40, then 25 × $40 = $1,000; the bond is trading at $1,000, producing a situation known as parity. Any time the market value of the bond equals the value of converted shares of stock, the situation is known as trading at parity. It could be said that the stock is at parity to the bond or the bond is at parity with the stock; both statements are correct.

As the conversion feature can be instituted only once per bond and flows only "one" way, (bonds into stock), the price of the bonds can be higher or equal to the converted value of the stock. If the bond market value ever falls below the converted common stock market value, a form of trading known as *arbitrage* or riskless arbitrage occurs.

Example: $1,000 Regal Corporation bonds are convertible into 25 shares of common stock. Due to the fact that interest rates have risen since the bonds were originally issued, the bonds are now trading at 75 or 75% of face (.75 × $1,000 = $750). What would the stock have to be trading at to be at parity? Answer: $750 ÷ 25 shares = $30 per share. Let's assume the stock rose in price above 30 to 30 1/8. Bond traders would buy the bonds, give conversion instructions to the firm's operation area, and immediately sell the stock. The bonds cost $750, the sale of the 25 shares of stock at 30 1/8 would produce $753.125 netting a $3.125 profit per $1,000 bond. While it may not be worth the effort for $3.125, traders usually transact business in the $100,000s, thereby producing $312.50 per $100,000 worth of bonds.

By buying the bonds, converting, and selling the stock, the trader puts demand on the bonds, raising its price which provides supply to the stock, thereby lowering its price. This will continue until parity is reached. Remember that the common stock and the bonds are trading in their own separate environments, so it is possible that the public's demand for the stock is stronger than the bond trader's supply; and therefore, the price of the stock does not fall, but continues to rise over time. Each time the converted value of the stock exceeds the market value of the bonds, this arbitrage takes place.

Convertibles

A form of corporate issue that some traders find attractive is known as *converts* or *convertible issues*. This feature, found in certain corporate bonds and preferred stocks, permits the security owner to convert or change from that issue to another issue of the issuing company. The most common issue that traders choose to convert into is *common stock.*

For example, the Le Sabre Corporation issues $1 million worth of debt (bonds) which is convertible at the option of the bondholders into 25,000 shares of common stock. The ratio given is that a $1,000 bond is convertible into 25 shares of common stock. Due to the convertible feature, the bond has two "lives"—one as a debt instrument, the other as a surrogate for the common stock.

As a bond, it will trade at a price that the marketplace perceives as fair. Brought into this equation is the bond's coupon rate, current and perceived interest rates, in general, the years the bond has until maturity, the issuer's financial strength, and the prospects for the issuer and the issuer's industry in the future.

As a surrogate for the common stock, the bond will reflect the common stock's value which is comprised of earnings, dividends, growth potential, the position of the issuer in the industry, the industry itself, as well as the market in general.

To the bondholder, the advantage of this type of instrument is that it will trade either at its market value (as a bond) or at its value (as a surrogate for the common stock), *whichever is higher.*

The value of this type of issue to the issuing corporation is twofold. One, if the company has growth potential and that potential will be reflected in its common stock market price over time, the company can issue the bond at a slightly lower interest cost than if the bond did not have this feature. Second, if the price of the stock rises to the point where bondholders would convert, the corporation would be relieved of debt as it gains more owners through conversion.

Generally, when convertibles are issued, the provision carries a parity price for the underlying bond which is way above the stock's or other issue's current market price. The term parity means a value at which the bond or preferred stock (and the convertible equivalent common stock) are equal. Let's re-examine an illustration given earlier using different calculations.

Example: A $1,000 RIP 8% CU FA–2008 bond is trading at 90 (90% of the face amount or $900 ($1,000 × .90 = $900)). The bond is convertible in 30 shares of stock. Unless the stock is trading at a price of at least $30 per share (30 shares × $30 = $900), it would not be worthwhile to convert it as the bondholder would be losing money. The stock would be trading at parity if it was trading at $30 per share.

If the bond was trading at 96 and the stock was trading at $32 per share, the stock would be at parity with the bond.

$$\$1,000 \times .96 = \$960$$

$$30 \text{ shares} \times 32 = 960$$

Trading at Parity

Stock will often trade below parity but seldom above parity. As stated earlier, a bond is issued because it appears to be the best capital raising vehicle available at the time. The investors are looking for a return on their investments (interest). The use of conversion feature is a "sweetener" to make the offering more attractive. If investors wanted to own shares in the company, they would simply buy the common stock instead of the bond. The convertible bond gives the investor the return of a bond with the possibility of capital appreciation because of the convertible feature.

While the underlying stock is below parity, the bond will trade at, and is priced by, bond standards. However, the traders are ever cognizant of the market value of the common stock. As the common stock rises in value and starts to approach parity, the traders begin to become interested in the stock.

As the stock's converted value approaches and rises above parity, a situation occurs which attracts arbitrageurs.

Arbitrageurs are traders who simultaneously purchase and sell the same or equal securities in such a way as to take advantage of price differences prevailing in separate markets with relatively low risk.

Example: A $1,000 WIP 8% JJ–2010 bond is trading at 88 ½ and the stock is trading at 22 ⅜. The bond is convertible into 40 shares of common stock. Arbitrageurs would buy the bonds (cost— $885), give instructions to the appropriate operations area in the firm to convert the bonds, and sell the equivalent (convertible) shares of common stock immediately (40 × 22 ⅜ = $895); thereby earning $10 per bond profit.

Naturally, the arbitrageur would not go through this process for one bond, but how about $1 million worth of bonds which would bring in a profit of $10,000.

As the arbitrageurs buy the bond, the demand causes the bond price to rise, and when they sell the common stock the supply may or may not generate enough downward pressure to depress the common stock price. The effect of the arbitrageur's sales depends on what other factors are influencing the common stock's market value. If this "new" supply of stock in the market-place can affect the stock's price, the arbitrageurs will continue to buy the bonds, convert, and sell the stock until the bond price and the converted stocks value are at parity (equal).

While the arbitrageurs are utilizing the conversion process, other traders are buying and selling the bonds. They, too, realize that as the stock continues to move up in value, it has to move the bond price up with it because of the arbitrageurs. They are also cognizant that these bonds are no longer being priced in the marketplace by bond standards but are, in fact, a surrogate for the stock and are reflecting the stock's market value.

In the above example, where the WIP bond was convertible into 40 shares of stock, if the common stock rose to $25 per share, what would the bond be trading at to be at parity? The correct answer is 100 or par (stock is $25 per share × 40 shares = $1,000). Even though this 8% bond, when priced by bond standards was worth approximately 88 ½, the conversion feature would cause its price to rise to 100. If the stock continues to move up in value, the bonds will follow to even higher levels.

Another aspect of convertible issues concerns the rate of return on the investment. In the example, where the 8% bond is convertible into 40 shares of common stock, if the bonds are paying 8% or $80 per $1,000 and the common stock was paying $2.00 per share per year, the income earned from the bond is the same as the common stock (8% of $1,000 = $80, $2 × 40 shares = $80). If the company increased the common stock dividend when the stock and the bond were at parity, it would "pay" the bond holders to convert into the common stock.

Dividends on common stock are declared by the Board of Directors of the corporation. Bond interest must be paid according to the bond's indenture. Sometimes a company will pay a special dividend or announce an increase in the rate of dividend. Either will affect the price of the common stock. If the traders perceive that such an event is about to happen and it will cause the price of the common stock to rise above parity of the bond, the traders will acquire the bonds and sell them after the arbitrageurs have implemented their strategy, which as stated before, causes the bond price to rise to parity.

Traders who specialize in the convertible security market must be adroit in two marketplaces—the bond market and the equity market. The more certain the marketplace is that a stock will break through parity, the sooner the bond price will start to reflect the anticipation. A trader must time that anticipation properly to be successful in trading the instrument.

SINKING FUND OR SINKER FEATURE

Certain bonds are issued with a clause that permits the issuing corporation to reacquire the debt in the open market and pay for it out of corporate earnings. This feature is known as the *sinker* or *sinking fund*. Most, if not all, sinking funds mandate that the acquisitions be made when the instruments are trading at below par and only within certain time periods. A corporate bond trader could "follow" corporations that have outstanding debt containing this feature and anticipate whether or not the sinker will "kick in." The trader starts to accumulate the issue at its current prices. If the sinker kicks in, the demand will impact the market price, enabling the trader to sell the bonds to the sinking fund operator at a profit. This process is risky, as interest rates could rise causing the value of the trader's position to fall or even worse, the corporation may decide not to evoke the sinker thereby leaving the corporate bond trader long (owner) of the bonds which must be sold into the marketplace.

Accurate assessment of a bond's value is important even in the process of bringing new issues to the market. New corporate debt issues are brought to market through negotiated underwritings. During these negotiations between corporate management and the underwriters, the coupon rates, maturity date, and price at which the bonds are to be issued at are set. When the new issue comes to market, traders have their own opinions as to what the price (yield) should be. When these new issues are finally released for trading, the traders take positions. If the issue is from a well-known corporation, it will trade on its name alone. Bonds of lesser known issues must be "sold" by security brokers. If the issue is believed to be overpriced, traders will sell; if it is underpriced, traders will buy. When the market value adjusts, the trades close out their positions. Traders will only profit from this approach when they are correct in their assessment of the bond's value. When their assessment is incorrect, they may suffer a loss.

THE FED'S ROLE IN CORPORATE BOND TRADING

Another approach to trading, used not only by corporate traders but other bond traders as well, is trying to determine what the Fed is going to do. The Fed is industry jargon for the Federal Reserve Board. Watching the Fed means guessing when it will take market action which will change interest rates in their ongoing monitoring of the economy. For example, each Monday, the Fed comes to market to issue new T Bills through an auction held with government dealer firms. The rates set at this time establish the tone for all debt trading over the near term. Besides the Fed market action, outside influences could affect interest rates such as fear of inflation which could send interest rates up. Fear of a slowdown in the economy could send rates down. Bond traders who watch the Fed look for indications as to which course of action the Fed may be taking. As the quote spread and mark-up on bonds are relatively small, any action by the Fed, either perceived or actual, would ripple through the entire marketplace causing a readjustment of prices and a profit or a loss to trader's position.

The Fed interacts with the market for many reasons other than monetary policy. It takes a keen eye and good understanding of the dynamics of the marketplace to be able to "read" the Fed. At the writing of this book, the "hot" buttons are corporate profits, balance of payments, and the dollar in international exchange. Any unexpected changes in the three, either individually or collectively, *may* cause Fed action which, in turn, may affect interest rates. The marketplace may anticipate Fed action and the rates of bonds may be affected whether or not the Fed takes action. The traders must accurately judge this if they are to be successful.

THE ROLE OF THE INTEREST FUTURES MARKET

Some corporate bond traders also watch the interest rate futures market, as these contracts tend to foretell the future. One of the most active is the T Bond future whose market is comprised of the opinions of many diverse and separate interests. It, therefore, can be a barometer of professional opinions and a helpful tool in a trader's assessment of "things to come." For those of you who are not familiar with the futures product, a *future contract* sets the price today at which a delivery is to take place in the *future.* If you buy a future today that is due for a delivery let's say in a year from now, the price you pay on delivery is the price you set for the future today. If you, however, sold that future, the price you sold the future at today is the price you will receive when you deliver the underlying product.

The perception of where interest rates are heading also affects the public's willingness to invest over time. If the perception is that interest rates will rise, the public will be unwilling to invest money in long-term instruments. Therefore, the price of long-term bond prices will become soft and perhaps fall while short-term instruments will rise. The effect is that the yields on short-term instruments will drop in comparison to long-term instruments. The difference in rates will magnify. If, on the other hand, the perception is that interest rates are going to fall, the investing public will want long-term instruments to lock in the higher rate, and the prices will increase causing the yields to fall.

If interest rates, from short term to long term, were to be charted, an interest rate "line" would be developed. This rate line will change over time as interest rates, or the perception thereof change. If the changes in these relationships can be anticipated accurately, traders will take positions from which profits would occur as the prices of the positioned instruments reflect these adjustments.

SUMMARY

Debt instruments of certain corporations are always tradable. The name of the issuer is a household word and ownership of these instruments is expected to be found in almost everyone's portfolio. Traders who have access to the segment of the marketplace represented by these clients try to keep an inventory that can satisfy the needs of buyers and anticipated sellers as well. The "adequate inventory" decision includes perception of interest rate movements, as well as other factors that affect bond prices. These popular and actively traded bonds are maintained in a trader's position in a similar fashion to an equity trader. What is popular? Which appeared in what article? Which issue appears to be improving its financial position? All of these questions play on the trader's mind while assuming different positions.

Chapter 7

Preferred Stock Traders

Preferred stocks are fixed income instruments with their own very unique environment. To understand the trading of these stocks, you must concentrate on the issue's properties. Some of the properties of preferred stocks are:

1. Stock represents ownership and not debt of the issuer.

2. Income is paid in the form of *dividends.*

3. Dividends must be paid from *corporate earnings* or *retained earnings.*

4. Dividends must be declared by the board of directors. If not paid—so what!!! The preferred shareholder is an owner.

5. Bonds pay interest, which is an expense to the company and must be paid whether or not the company has any earnings. In addition, bondholders can foreclose on the company if interest is not paid.

6. The reason why the broad category known as preferred stock is referred to as a fixed income security is that the issue *is to pay a fixed rate of dividend per share, per year.*

As an instrument that is to pay a fixed dividend per share, per year, the preferred trader must be concerned with the movement of interest rates. As with any interest-rate sensitive instrument, as interest rates rise, the market value of these instruments will fall, and vice versa. Depending on the traders' perception of the direction rates are taking, traders will control the size of their trading positions.

Preferred stock descriptions display the rate of dividends one of two ways—either as a percent or as a dollar figure. Therefore, a company which has issued preferred stock may have it displayed as 8% preferred or $8 preferred. These are *not* the same, as the 8% is to pay 8% of the preferred stock's par value, whereas the $8 preferred is simply supposed to pay $8 per share, per year.

Par value is a value assigned to shares of stock which permits the company to convert shares to dollars on the corporate Balance Sheet. It has no relationship to market value. For example, 10 people invest $10,000 each into a new business corporation. The net worth of the business at that point is $100,000 ($10 \times $10,000). Against the investment, the 10 people take equal numbers of shares of stock to represent their investment. As the 100 shares are trading in a *round lot,* they decide to take 100 shares each. A round lot is a unit of trading or multiple thereof. Stocks are traded in round lots of 100 shares for active stocks and 10 shares for high priced, inactive ones. The 10 people, therefore, took 1,000 shares in total to represent the $100,000 investment. The company's Balance Sheet would show the line item as 1,000 shares common stock equals $100,000. Any accountant would ask how did the shares (apples) equate to dollars (oranges)? Or why the mixture of apples and oranges? To convert shares to dollars, a conduit is needed. That conduit is par value; $100,000 ÷ 1,000 shares = $100

par value. The Balance Sheet would read 1,000 shares par value
$100 = $100,000.

In the above example, the investors could have just as easily
taken 10,000 shares apiece, which would have resulted in the
initial par value being only $10. There is no hard or fast rule
governing the amount of what a stock's par value should be.

A *percent preferred payment* means to pay that percent of its
par value. For a trader (or anyone else for that matter) it is imperative that the par value be known in order to compute yield based
on the income based on dividend. For instance, an 8% preferred
stock with a $100 par value is supposed to pay $8 per share, per
year. If the preferred stock had a $50 par value, it would pay $4;
whereas a $10 par value would pay 80 cents. Each of these cases
would result in a different fair market price for each issue. Add to
this the fact that these relationships only exist if a corporation's
board of directors decides to continuously pay the dividend.

FOUR FEATURES OF PREFERRED STOCK

In addition to the preferred's dividend rate, four features
affect the market value of preferred issues that may or may not be
present in any given particular issue. These features are that the
issues are:

1. Cumulative;

2. Participating;

3. Callable; and

4. Convertible.

Cumulative Preferred Stock

A *cumulative preferred issue* is one in which dividends,
which are not paid, accumulate and must eventually be paid
before the common stockholder can receive any dividend distribution. This feature offers an entire new dimension to trading a
product. For example, a company has an $8 preferred stock

outstanding. The preferred is supposed to pay $8 per year or $2 per quarter. For the last 3 years, the management has decided to conserve cash and omit the dividend. Now with $24 of accrued dividend and the first quarter dividend of $2 coming due (for a total of $26), the belief is that the company will pay "something." A trader that can correctly assess that "something" could profit by properly positioning the issue.

Paying Dividends. First and most important, the dividend is owed by the company to the shareholder. It will be paid to the shareholder of record at the time the dividend is declared. It is *not* owed to the shareholder who owned the security at the time the dividend passed (omitted).

The preferred issue in discussion has not paid a dividend in 3 years and is priced primarily on income expectation and the success, of lack of same, of the issuing company. Suppose an $8 preferred issued by a similar company to the one paying the dividend is trading at approximately $80 per share. Its current yield would be 10% ($80 ÷ $8 = 10%). The issue under discussion would naturally be selling for less, as it has not paid a dividend for 3 years. However, consider that the company has had consistently good earnings over the period and may now begin to pay out cash, in the form of dividends, to the preferred stockholders.

If the preferred issue under consideration was a noncumulative preferred issue (meaning that once a dividend was passed and not collected, it would be lost forever), the preferred stock trader could assume that if the quarterly dividend is paid it will be somewhere between $0 and $2 ($2 per quarter × 4 = $8 per year). However, in the aforementioned case, the dividend could be anywhere from $0 to $26 ($2 for the quarter plus $24 in accruals). What would be a fair market price then? If an $8 preferred is worth $80, what is the $32 preferred worth ($26 plus $2 per quarter for the remaining three quarters, or $24 in accruals plus $2 for the first quarter equals $26 plus the expectation of $2 each quarter for the remaining quarters)?

Determining Fair Market Value. Assume you are the trader and believe that the firm will not pay the $26 all at once. If this is true, then they may pay the remaining dividends over the remaining quarters of the fourth year. The result is the same in that at the end of the year all preferred dividends (both current and in arrears) have been paid, giving the shareowner $32 on an investment of $ _?_ . The "?" is the big question—this is the fair market value.

As the possibility of the company "cleaning up" its arrears becomes more realistic, speculators will enter the marketplace trying to outguess and/or outmaneuver the rest. Their acquisition of the issue would cause the preferred stock to become active, perking up the interests of traders. As this cycle continues, the preferred's market value will rise. Traders going in and out of position will try to maintain a stance that will allow them to, perhaps, earn a profit from two sources. The first source would be the spread between their bid and offer and the second would be the rise in the stock's market value that is forming the basis of a long position. If the traders position the issue, they must be careful not to "ride" it up "too far" in value. If the rumor or perception or "gut feeling" proves to be either wrong or overestimated, the value of the stock will fall rapidly, leaving the trader with a good possibility of a loss.

Besides determining what the perceived fair market value of the issue is prior to accrued dividend distribution, traders must also assess fair market value during and after the dividend distribution. Each part of the process is equally important in establishing fair market value. The fact that they owe $24 in arrears is only as important as how long it will take to pay off the arrears (one time, 1 year, 2 years, or longer), and what is the company expecting to do after they pay accruals. In other words, is the company in a windfall position paying dividends from unexpected earnings which, after a comparatively brief period of time, will fall back to accruing arrears? Or will it now continue to pay its obligations so that the preferred issue may be calculated as an $8 fixed income security? The market's perception of what the company will do will determine the market value. Traders may trade with or against this market sentiment.

Participating Preferred Stock

Another feature that a preferred issue may have is known as a *participation clause*. This feature establishes the conditions under which the preferred issue will share in additional dividend payments along with the common stockholder. Each participation feature is unique to each affected preferred.

Example: M. Shoe Company has a $9 participating preferred outstanding that permits the preferred shareholder to receive an additional 50 cents in dividends for every dollar of dividend the common shareholder receives in excess of a $9 per share payment. In other words, the preferred shareholder is paid $9 per share dividend first, then the common shareholder can be paid up to $9 after which for every $1 paid to the common shareholder, 50 cents must be paid to the preferred shareholder.

Determining the Fair Market Value. Evaluating the market value of this type of preferred issue includes the possibility or reality of that extra dividend being paid. Has the company had a history of doing this? What is the company's attitude on dividend payouts? What is the largest amount of cash dividend ever paid to the common shareholder up until now?

Another approach to understanding participating preferred issues is to understand that when the preferred was issued, it was possible that the common stockholder was receiving a lot less than the $9 mentioned in the participation feature in our example. However, M. Shoe Company has grown and the payment of dividends has not only become a permanent part of company policy, but the amount paid has grown as well. The company has been paying close to $9 per year for the last few years, and it is possible that this particular preferred feature may "kick in" soon. As a preferred trader, you would try to anticipate the company's policy and position the preferred stock accordingly. Again, you could trade in and out of the market or commit capital and "work" a position. You could get a profit by trading the spread of the quote. A second alternative not only gives profit through the width of the quote, but also the opportunity to profit from correctly estimating where the value of the stock will be after certain events do or do not happen.

Remember, in both the cumulative and participating preferred issues, the dividends must be declared by the board of directors of the company. If, in the case of the aforementioned participating preferred stock, the directors never declare a dividend payment to the common shareholders for more than $9 per share, per year, the preferred will never earn more than $9 regardless of how much the company earns. The participation feature is, in this case, an illusion.

Callable Preferred Stock

Another type of preferred that traders watch carefully are callable preferred issues. These preferred issues may be retired (called in) at the direction of the issuer. Usually the preferred will be called when the company can obtain financing at more reasonable (lower) rates. The issuer uses the proceeds from the new, less expensive instruments to pay off the older, more expensive issue.

Callable features exist in some debt instruments as well. Corporate, municipal, and U.S. government issues may have callable debt instrument features. The callable preferred issues must be viewed from a different perspective than callable debt issues. This is due to the different tax implications of dividends and interest for both issues.

Interest is an expense to the firm, whereas dividends are paid from after-tax earnings. This difference is of major importance to the company as it has to pay taxes on earnings in either case and after-tax earnings are clearly the better choice. Let's look at an example to better understand the difference.

Example: Ponte D'Or's profit and loss statement reads as follows:

	Exhibit 1	*Exhibit 2*
Sales	$2.00	$2.00
Interest expense	−1.00	—
Before tax	$1.00	$2.00
Tax (50%)	− .50	−1.00
	$ .50	$1.00
Preferred dividend	—	−1.00
	$ .50	0

In Exhibit 1, the company paid its interest expense and paid 50 cents in income tax, leaving 50 cents as post-tax earnings. In Exhibit 2, the company paid $1 in income tax (twice as much as in Exhibit 1) and paid $1 in dividends (instead of as interest), thereby depleting its earnings.

To turn the picture another way, a company needs $1 of revenue for $1 of expense, yet needs $2 of revenue for $1 of dividend (given a 50% tax rate, the other $1 will be paid in taxes). It is, therefore, less "expensive" for a company to pay a $1 interest than it would be $1 of dividend. Following this scenario, a company may be better off by calling in its preferred stock by issuing debt.

The problem with callable issues that are interest-rate sensitive is that their prices rise when interest rates fall, making it attractive for the issuer to replace the issue with less expensive "money." This is the worst time for the bondholder or shareholder, as the ability to reinvest at the previous rates of return are no longer existent at that safety level.

In the case of the preferred trader, the possibility of an issue being called not only exists when overall interest rates fall, but also when switched from equity ownership to debt in order to benefit the company and/or the voting common stockholders.

Convertible Preferred Stock

Convertible preferred issues are issues where the owner may exchange his issues for a specified number of shares of stock. Interest paid on such issues is lower than the usual interest rate for straight debt issues. Convertible issues are discussed at length in Chapter 6.

SUMMARY

The world of the preferred trader is different from that of other traders. Not only must the trader follow interest rates, but he must understand the features that may be affecting that particular issue. Take for example, if a trader is called and asked to make a bid on a particular issue, the trader better familiarize himself with that issue in order to make a valid quote. If the trader bids too low, the potential seller will go elsewhere; if the trader bids too high, forget it!

To recap, the world of the preferred trader is different from other issues traders because:

1. Like common stock, preferred stock represents ownership; but *unlike* common stock, preferred stock is generally considered a fixed income instrument.

2. Like bonds, preferred stocks are fixed income instruments; but unlike bonds, payment of income (dividends) does not have to be made (interest).

3. Like bonds, the dividend rate of a preferred stock is dependent on such factors as the current interest rate climate and the strength of the issuer. Unlike debt, the dividend rate may be offset by features such as cumulative or participating issues (e.g., an $8 preferred that does not pay its dividend on a regular basis may be worth more or less in the marketplace than a 4% preferred that pays every quarter period. A 4% preferred of a $100 par value preferred may be worth more or less than a 6% preferred with a par value of $50. A preferred with a cumulative feature only has meaning if the company has the ability to pay the dividend owed. A participating feature has value in the marketplace only if the company has the ability to earn sufficient amounts to make the feature workable.

Review all of the above-listed items with the usual pricing tests for all issues (such as the financial strength of the issuer, the current interest rate trends, and so on) and you have a better understanding of the world of the preferred stock trader.

Chapter 8

Municipal Issues Traders

State and local government come to the marketplace to borrow money for a multitude of purposes. The vehicles used to raise that money are known as *municipal issues.* These securities are issued in the form of *bonds* (long term) or *notes* (short term). The most distinguishing characteristic of these instruments is that the interest paid to the debtholder on most of these instruments is not subject to Federal income tax. If the owner resides within the state of issuance, the interest paid on the issue is not subject to state and local taxes, either.

In dealing with these instruments, traders must remember that this nontaxable feature becomes more and more important as the tax rates charged within the states, cities, and localities therein increases. As these instruments are fixed income securities, they compete head on with corporate and U.S. Treasury instruments whose interest is fully taxable by the Federal government. The interest paid on U.S. Treasury instruments is free from state and local taxes, however. The tax liability plays a major factor in pricing the issues.

Another distinguishing characteristic is that (with only a few exceptions) municipal offerings are small in size as compared to corporate and government debt issues. Due to this fact, the trading methodology in municipal securities differs from that of other instruments. These instruments trade on a yield-to-maturity basis known as *basis prices.*

Yield-to-maturity basis is a phrase used to explain the price discovery used in municipal bonds. As most municipals are transacted based on the nomenclature of the bond, participants in the transaction are interested in the yield-to-maturity. When the yield-to-maturity is compared to the coupon rate of the instrument, the actual dollar price can be fairly and accurately guesstimated.

Example: N.Y. State Thruways 8% 20-year debt at a yield-to-maturity of 8.94 or, the correct way of saying the same thing, N.Y. State Thruway's 8's at 8.94 basis, would have a price about 100 points below par.

$$\begin{array}{r} \$1,000 \text{ Mat} \\ \underline{900 \text{ @MV}} \\ 100 \text{ appreciation} \end{array}$$

$$\$100/20 \text{ years} = \$5 \text{ per year}$$

$$\frac{80+5}{\dfrac{(1000+900)}{2}} = \frac{85}{950} = 8.94$$

The typical municipal request includes state of issuance, duration, rating, and level of financial accountability. The investor is not interested in a particular issue but any one of a group of issues that satisfies the need. Therefore, when the bonds that meet the stated standards are quoted, they are quoted on a yield-to-maturity basis or at a basis price.

Example:

Port Authority of N.Y. & N.J. 7% of 11-1-2011 @ 7.04
Port Authority of N.Y. & N.J. 6⅞% of 1-1-2025 @ 7.33
Port Authority of N.Y. & N.J. 7% of 9-1-2024 @ 7.41

As the basis price for each of these bonds is slightly greater than the coupon rate, the dollar equivalent price must be slightly below par and is $955.00, $942.50, and $948.75 per $1,000 of debt, respectively.

The tax obligation and the issue size mentioned above results in a concentrated investment interest in many small issues rather than the investment interest being spread over a few large ones. You may better understand this concept if we review the history of a typical municipal offering.

ISSUING A MUNICIPAL SECURITY

A usual municipal offering comes to the market through a financing mechanism known as *competitive underwritings.* Competitive underwriting takes place through a sealed envelope bidding process employed by various underwriting groups interested in handling the distribution of a securities issue. The contract is awarded to one group by the issuer on the basis of the highest price paid, interest rate expense, and tax considerations. The new issue is offered for sale and it has component parts maturing at different dates. This is known as serial offering. After the particular series is placed (sold), it disappears from the market. Over the lifespan of the particular issue, parts of it may return to the marketplace to be traded again only to disappear from the marketplace again. Unlike the much larger corporate and treasury issues, there is no continuous trading of this one particular issue. Therefore, an individual purchasing a particular issue on one day, may not be able to buy the same issue on another date. The pricing of each individual issue must be made at the time it becomes available in the marketplace.

To assist in this pricing procedure, municipal issuers and their issues are rated by various rating services. Among the most popular rating services used are Moody's and Standard & Poor's.

These services, using various criteria, measure the issuer's or issue's financial strength and their ability to meet their interest and principal obligation. To summarize, a given locale can have many different issues outstanding, different tax or fee zones, and different ratings.

The ability of an issuer to pay interest and return principal at maturity also affects the rating of the instrument. The avenues open to the issuer to collect these funds is set forth in part of the issues description.

FOUR TYPES OF AVAILABLE MUNICIPALS

The different municipal securities available are as follows:

General Obligation (GO) *Bond.* A bond carrying a GO designation will have its interest and principal paid from the full taxing power of the issuer. The ability of the issuer to collect taxes from any source directly affects the rating. In this case, the ability of the issuer is directly related to the tax base of municipality.

Revenue (Rev) *Bond.* A bond bearing this description is supported from the revenue earned from a particular project. A toll road, turnpike, thruway, and so on are all examples of such a project. The strength of the project will determine the safety of the issue. For example, even if a toll road saves time, the majority of traffic may choose a "free road" nearby though it takes a little longer.

Limited Tax (LT) *Bond.* Issues supported by limited taxes refers to the issuer collecting a specified tax, for example, a cigarette tax or a sales tax. The ability of the issuer to collect the special tax affects the rating of the issue. For example, a bond issued 20 years ago and having 10 years remaining could be in trouble if it was backed by a tax collection based on 70 to 80% of the area's adult population smoking cigarettes. Today's adult population does not smoke in the same proportions as did the adult population of 10 years ago.

Industrial Revenue (Ind Rev) *Bond.* These bonds are either for the purpose of an industrial effort or are backed by an industrial effort. Because it is for the benefit of an industrial entity, the U.S. Internal Revenue Service may negate the issue's tax-free status, and rule that the interest paid on the debt is fully taxable as a corporate issue.

At this point in our discussion of municipals, you can start to appreciate the amount of product knowledge that a municipal trader must have in order to operate and succeed. The different types of municipals available only scratches the surface of what a trader should know.

WHAT A TRADER SHOULD KNOW ABOUT MUNICIPAL ISSUES

There are many other subtle differences which the trader should understand and use to his advantage.

Due to the interest on a municipal being nontaxable, the income tax levels of the various states and localities play an important role in setting the issue's coupon rate. This, in turn, has an effect on the pricing of the issue. An issuer of municipal debt representing a low or no income tax locale has a different problem setting coupon or interest rate than does one from a higher tax area.

Example: Within a given state there is the city of Randopolis which has a 2% income tax. Elsewhere in the same state is the town of Craigville which does not have an income tax. Craigville's government, when considering rates of interest for new debt issues, must realize the adjustment below equivalent corporate rates. If the break-even tax rate between corporate and municipal is 30% and if the equivalent corporate bond rate being issued has a 10% coupon rate, the muni could be issued with a 7% coupon rate. From an income tax standpoint the bonds are equal. This 7% coupon rate is figured as follows.

$$\begin{array}{rl} 100\% & \text{Income} \\ -\ 30\% & \text{Tax rate} \\ \hline 70\% & \text{Net income} \end{array}$$

$$\frac{10\%}{x} \times \frac{100\%}{70\%}$$

$$100\%\ x = 700\%$$

$$x = 7\%$$

A $1,000 corporate bond, carrying a 10% coupon rate will pay $100 in interest per year. If the federal income tax was 25% and the state income taxes were 5% for a total of 30%, $30 of the interest will go to income taxes. Seventy dollars is thereby retained by the bondholder. The purchaser of a $1,000 Craigville 7% bond would receive $70 interest and retain all of it.

Randopolis has a 2% income tax, so the income tax break-even point, based on the above calculations should be 32%. Randopolis should be able to issue a municipal bond equal to the 10% corporate bond with a coupon rate of 6.8%.

The $1,000 corporate bond, which pays 10% interest, will pay $100. The resident of Randopolis will retain $68, as $32 of the $100 must be paid out to the federal, state, and local authorities.

As these are municipal securities, interest income from debt instruments issued anywhere within the state are free from state and local taxes. As the income received is tax free, a resident of the state would pay no income tax on the interest earned. It makes a difference to the purchaser if all instruments were issued at their full taxability rate. Let's take a look at three different issues and see how a resident of Craigville would make out if he considered buying one of these three issues.

Corporate Bond—Regal Corporation—

The issue is 100% taxable with a 10% coupon rate equal to $100 per $1,000 of interest earned. If this issue was owned by an individual in the highest tax bracket of Craigville, 30% would go to income tax leaving that individual with only $70.

If owned by an individual in the highest tax bracket in Randopolis, the individual would pay 30% federal and state income tax and 2% city tax, totaling 32%. This leaves the bondholder only $68.

Debt instruments issued by either Craigville, Randopolis, another municipality within the state, or the state itself—

Any of these issues would carry a 7 1/2% coupon and will net the owner $75 per $1,000 as federal, state, and local (in the case of Randopolis) income taxes are not applicable on the interest earned.

Debt instruments issued by another state and purchased by an individual in Craigville—

This individual is in the maximum tax bracket and resides in Craigville but he will keep 2% more of the interest income than will an individual buying the same issue who resides in Randopolis.

These subtle differences between issues are major points in a municipal trader's life. In the above examples, it would appear that against Regal Corporation's 10% issue, Randopolis could issue a 6.8% debt instrument as the individuals who reside in Randopolis would have to pay 32% of the income tax earned to federal, state, and local governments. However, the resident of Randopolis could also purchase debt issued by Craigville and have the same tax-free status. Therefore, the Randopolis resident could receive 7% on the Craigville instrument or 6.8% on the Randopolis instrument. Which would you choose? This ability by investors to choose has a direct effect on the issuers and the traders of the instruments.

BASIS PRICE: THE FOUNDATION FOR ALL MUNICIPAL ISSUES

With all of the above named differences, nuances, and idiosyncrasies, municipal securities trade and trade well. Firms specialize in this product and their clients are, in most cases, considered astute investors. Therefore, to "melt down" all of these complexities into a cohesive product, a common denominator must be brought into play. That denominator is known as basis price.

Most municipal issues trade at basis prices. The term is synonymous with yield to maturity. If the municipal issue is purchased and held to maturity, the return the investor would receive is known as the *yield to maturity.*

Example: Assume an investor, Patty Gordon, purchased a $1,000 bond for $900 plus accrued interest. The bond is a 20-year bond carrying an 8% coupon.

What is known is as follows. Patty is paying $900 for a debt whose issuer will pay $1,000 20 years from now when one bond matures. Patty will have a gain of $100. Patty will be receiving $80 per year interest income per $1,000 instrument. Good accounting practice states that the $100 gain must be spread out over the life of the instrument. As this is a 20-year bond, the computation works out to $5 per year. ($100/20 = $5.) If the instrument is at a discount, the term for "spreading out" the difference is *amortizing*. If the bond is at a premium, the term is *depleting*. The sum being amortized is added to the dollar amount of interest being received per year; if the sum is being depleted, it is subtracted from the interest received.

Taking into account the amortization factor, this part of the formula would read $80 + $5 = $85. As the instrument is being amortized at $5 per year, that accrual must be reflected someplace. The most logical place is to have it added to the market value ($900 + $5 for the first year, $900 + $10 for the second year, $900 + $50 for the tenth year, and $900 + $100 for the twentieth year). So, $900 + $100 = $1,000, which is the *face amount* received by the bondholder at maturity.

As the instrument in the above example is increasing at $5 per year, for half of its 20-year life, its value (not its market value) on "paper" will be $950 or less. For the second half, it will be greater than $950. To calculate this yield we must seek an average value of the issue. It is calculated as follows:

$$
\begin{array}{ll}
\text{Cost price} & \$\ \ 900 \\
+ \text{ Value at maturity} & \underline{\$1,000} \\
& \$1,900
\end{array}
$$

$$\$1,900/2 = \$950 \text{ average value}$$

The following method to calculate yield to maturity is known as the *rule of thumb:*

$$
\frac{\substack{\text{Annual interest} \ + \text{Annual amortized value} \\ \text{income} \quad\ \ - \text{Annual depleted value}}}{\left(\dfrac{\text{Current market value} + \text{Value at maturity}}{2}\right)}
$$

$$\frac{80 + 5}{\left(\dfrac{900 + 1{,}000}{2}\right)} = \frac{85}{950} = 8.95$$

The yield to maturity or basis price for this bond is 8.95.

Let's run through another example, this time with a 30-year bond trading at a premium. The bond carries an 11% coupon and is currently trading at $1,300 per $1,000 debt.

Current market value $1,300 per $1,000
Value at maturity $1,000
                         $ 300

$300/80 years = $10 per year

$$\left(\frac{\text{Interest income} - \text{Yearly depleted value}}{\dfrac{\text{Current market value} + \text{Value at maturity}}{2}}\right)$$

$$= \frac{\$110 - 10}{\left(\dfrac{\$1{,}300 + \$1{,}000}{2}\right)} - \frac{100}{\left(\dfrac{\$2{,}300}{2}\right)} - \frac{100}{\$1{,}150} = 8.70$$

The yield to maturity or basis price is 8.70.

While a few municipal issues trade at "dollar" prices as do corporate issues, the majority trade at basis prices. Normally, they trade at .05 or "nickel" intervals. It is this finely tuned price neutralizer that accounts for differences between issues.

HOW MUNICIPALS ARE QUOTED

When municipal traders quote these instruments, the quotes are made in basis point description. For example, the issue Marnee College Dormitory 8% FA–2006 is quoted at 8.10–7.90. Note that the bid is higher than the offer. If this was a "dollar" quote, the bid being higher than the offer would be in error. It would mean that the trader is willing to purchase the instrument at a higher price than he is willing to sell. The quote, as a yield to maturity presentation, is correct.

The instruments are issued with a fixed rate of interest, to be paid during the life of the instrument. During the instrument's life interest rates will change. For the instrument to retain its trading ability, its "rate" must remain competitive. Therefore, something must "give," as the debt's interest or coupon rates are not adjustable, the price must "give" way. Thus the question is not what the coupon rate is, but what is the return on investment. As stated earlier, current yield is cost price divided into annual interest amount to be received. Yield-to-maturity includes the amortization or depletion of the discount or premium.

The less "dollars" being paid to receive a finite sum of the debt by interest, the higher the yield. The more dollars, the lower the yield. In the above example, a quote of 8.10–7.90 on an 8% instrument would mean a bid of slightly below par and an offer slightly above par.

This can easily be displayed by using the correct yield formula. Here are some examples using a $1,000 bond which is carrying a 9% coupon and three prices—98, par (100), and 102:

$$\$1,000 \times .09 = \$90 = 90/980 = 9.18\%$$
$$= 90/1000 = 9.00\%$$
$$= 90/1020 = 8.82\%$$

If *you* were to apply the rule of thumb method for yield-to-maturity and apply these prices, the same relationship would be borne out. The lower the price, the higher the yield and vice versa.

Municipal bond traders look at the multitude of issues before them and by relating each instrument's coupon rate to the instrument's respective basis price, they do, almost subconsciously, a conversion to dollars. It is within this environment that trading is conducted.

PRICE TO CALL FEATURE

Price to call is a unique feature of basis price instruments. This concept involves callable debt instruments. To digress for a moment, callable instruments are those that can be retired at the will of the issuer under the terms outlined in the instrument's indenture. Generally, this feature carries the dates on which the instrument can be retired and the prices the issuer will have to pay if the instrument is so called.

Example: Let's assume Laughlinton issues an 8%, 30-year debt that is callable at 102 after 10 years. If the bonds were trading at par, the yield to maturity would be 8%.

$$\frac{80 \pm 0}{\left(\dfrac{\$1,000 + \$1,000}{2}\right)} = \frac{80}{\$1,000} = .8 = 8\%$$

However, the price to call would yield:

$1,020   Call price
$1,000   Current market value
$ 20

$$\$20/10 = 2$$

$$\frac{80 + 2}{\left(\dfrac{\$1,020 + \$1,000}{2}\right)} = \frac{82}{\$1,010} = 8.11$$

When trading with the public, the municipal trader must quote the municipals at the yield to maturity or price to call rate, whichever is lower. This is important as there is no guarantee that a municipality will call the debt and/or when that municipality will retire the issue. Therefore, the public must be given the "worst" of all market yields. Municipal traders make themselves sensitive to when issues may or may not be called. The term used is *sensitive,* not *psychic.* Therefore, they are occasionally wrong.

As stated throughout this book, as interest rates fall, bond prices rise, yields fall, and vice versa. Therefore, as interest rates in the marketplace fall, the value of outstanding issues increases. Thus it is possible that the market price of a bond may rise above the call price. However, as interest rates fall, the municipality is cognizant of its ability to retire old, higher interest-rate paying bonds with lower rate bonds for less cost. If they call the bond, the bondholder will receive the call price and not the market price for the bonds.

Traders, therefore, try to determine which bonds selling below the call price may be called and they will try to buy them. Bonds trading above call are either sold or shied away from. Traders are also cognizant of the disparity between the market price and the price to call. If the difference grows to the point that the risk of call exceeds the profit potential, traders will not hold these issues in position.

SPECIFIED/UNSPECIFIED FEATURE

Uncommon in most other instruments, but found in municipal securities, is the ability for an issuer to borrow funds for different purposes. Each purpose will be *specified* on each instrument. To better explain this concept, suppose a municipality, we'll call it the city of Grandton, issues debt instruments to assist in the financing of four different high school districts. The issuing authority stands equally behind each of the four purposes and yet, in certain states, each separate purpose must be so stated on the instrument. The city of Grandton, in this case, would have to issue municipal debt stating which high school district was to benefit from which of the debt issues. While the issues are all equal, the fact that the instruments carry different descriptions causes concern to those unindoctrinated with the instrument.

To traders, the issuer, its financial condition, and the terms of issue are important and not the high school districts. Therefore, these issues trade *unspecified*. This term means that whichever instrument of the issue is delivered against settlement would be accepted as a good delivery for the investor. Traders must be cautious, though, of times when issues may be traded unspecified when they truly should be specified.

At times, issues of the same municipality and for the same or similar types of purposes, which are equal, will trade at the same basis price for long periods of time. Those who become involved with these instruments eventually accept them as being traded unspecified. Everything is copesetic until some event occurs that changes this relationship. Such a change could cause the bond to go down in value. At that time, costly problems exist as everyone claims to have owned or traded the more expensive of the two issues.

THE BLUE LIST

As stated earlier in this chapter, municipal offerings are often issued in serial form. While the initial offering is usually large in size, the multiple maturity dates make the individual series seem small. The issue is offered, then sold, and then disappears from the market. Therefore, a specific issue which was available yesterday may not be available today. Issues available today will not be available tomorrow. These same issues were probably not available yesterday.

Municipal traders, therefore, operate in a limited environment. Their parameters generally encompass the states in which their firm maintains offices or investment banking relationships. Through these conduits, the traders carry on business relationships. Occasionally, there is a need for special handling of a situation. Examples of these situations would be:

A client wants to acquire a muni issue which is not usually part of the trader's positions.

A client wants to sell a muni issue for which the trader does not have a ready market (e.g., bond issues offered by a state in which the trader's firm does not maintain a facility).

A trader has "taken down" an acquired position which is larger than the trader's contacts (branches) can absorb.

A trader believes that a better price can be obtained outside the trader's usual environment.

A client requests the use of an intermediary to disguise the fact that the client is selling an issue. This necessitates the use of a broker's broker or dealer's broker to interject itself between the buyer and the seller. The blue sheets carry such a list of names.

Figure 8.1. The Blue List.

Amt. M	Security	Purpose	Rate	Maturity	Yield or Price	Offered By
	ALABAMA					
+ 10	ALABAMA ST		4.500	11/01/89	6.25	GiantReC
25	ALABAMA ST		12.000	12/01/89	6.30	StoneFor
230	ALABAMA ST		4.500	06/01/90	6.75	ONiel&Pr
+ 550	ALABAMA HIGHER ED LN CORP	LOC FUJI	6.400	03/01/92	100	Overland
250	ALABAMA HSG FIN AUTH SINGLE		0.000	10/01/14	9.50	Beddings
1000	ALABAMA HSG FIN AUTH SINGLE		0.000	10/01/14	9.50	ReidWrig
5	ALABAMA ST CORRECTIONS INSTN		7.200	04/01/95	6.70	GiantReC
30	ALABAMA ST DOCKS DEPT COAL REV	P/R @ 103	10.000	10/01/00 C95	6.75	GiantReC
+ 5	ALABAMA ST HWY AUTH REV		5.000	11/01/89 ETM	6.25	Slogger
+1000	ALABAMA ST MUN ELEC AUTH PWR		7.000	09/01/93	6.70	SwiftArr
+1250	ALABAMA ST PUB SCH & COLLEGE	SER.N	5.500	05/01/92 ETM	6.60	FirstLiv
1125	ALABAMA ST PUB SCH & COLLEGE (CA @ 101½)		6.700	11/01/98 C95 #	6.80	LEFANT
1000	ALABAMA ST PUB SCH & COLLEGE	CA @ 100	6.750	11/01/00 C98 #	6.90	StoneFor
+ 10	ALABAMA ST UNIV REV		5.700	12/01/00	7.20	Overland
135	ALEXANDER CITY ALA UTIL REV	BK.QD	6.500	12/01/92	100	StoneFor
95	ALEXANDER CITY ALA UTIL REV	BK.QD	6.600	12/01/93	100	LEFANT
70	ALEXANDER CITY ALA UTIL REV	BK.QD	6.700	12/01/94	100	ONiel&Pr
50	ALEXANDER CITY ALA UTIL REV	BK.QD	6.900	12/01/96	100	DowneDTv
75	ALEXANDER CITY ALA UTIL REV	BK.QD	6.950	12/01/97	100	PointerD
80	ALEXANDER CITY ALA UTIL REV	BK.QD	7.050	12/01/99	100	StoneFor
110	ALEXANDER CITY ALA UTIL REV	BK.QD	7.100	12/01/00	100	FirstCont
235	ALEXANDER CITY ALA UTIL REV	BK.QD	7.150	12/01/01	100	NIKE REP
50	BIRMINGHAM ALA INDL WTR BRD		6.000	07/01/07 ETM	7.10	DaisyCh

+ 700	BIRMINGHAM ALA INDL WTR BRD		6.200	07/01/08 ETM	7.10	FirstCont
15	BIRMINGHAM ALA NORTH MED (SINKING FUND 10/1/89)		6.375	04/01/99 ETM	6.60	PointerD
95	BIRMINGHAM ALA SPL CARE FACS BAPTIST MED CTRS SER B		8.600	04/01/94	6.75	
220	BIRMINGHAM ALA WTRWKS BRD WTR	MBIA	7.900	01/01/96	6.60	LEFANT
25	BIRMINGHAM BAPTIST MED CTR ALA		6.700	08/01/97	100	BeatDun
150	BIRMINGHAM JEFFERSON ALA CIVIC		5.500	09/01/90 ETM	6.20	StoneFor
840	BIRMINGHAM JEFFERSON ALA CIVIC		7.400	01/01/08	98 7/8	LEFANT
50	COURTLAND ALA INDL DEV BRD (CHAMPION INTL.)		5.750	11/01/97	95	Hill&Dole
635	DECATUR ALA INDL DEV BRD	MONSANTO CO	7.000	07/01/90	6.50	SatinEm
655	DECATUR ALA INDL DEV BRD	MONSANTO	7.000	07/01/90	6.50	CBCraigC
10	DOTHAN ALA		5.300	05/01/93 ETM	6.40	DowneDTv
	NEW YORK					
20	NEW YORK ST ENERGY RESH & DEV (ROCHESTER GAS/ELEC)	AMT PUT @ 100	5.875	07/15/27 P90 #	6.50	StoneFor
125	NEW YORK ST ENERGY RESH & DEV (CENTRAL HUDSON GAS/ELEC)	AMT	8.375	12/01/28	7.80	GiantReC
100	NEW YORK ST ENVIRONMENTAL FACS	AMT AMBAC	8.000	08/01/18	7.40	BeddPill
20	NEW YORK ST ENVIRONMENTAL FACS	AMT	8.000	08/01/18	103	DowneDTv
+ 10	NEW YORK ST HSG FIN AGY	ST UNIV	3.600	05/01/90	6.75	Ripperof
+ 15	NEW YORK ST HSG FIN AGY (LOC BANKERS TRUST) (HOMELESS)	*REG*	4.700	05/01/91 N/C	6.65	StoneForr.

+ Items so marked did not appear in the previous issue of The Blue List.

#Prices so marked are changed from the previous issue.

c Items so marked are reported to have call or option features. Consult offering house for full details.

Figure 8.1. (Continued)

Amt. M	Security	Purpose	Rate	Maturity		Yield or Price	Offered By
30	NEW YORK ST HSG FIN AGY	HLTH FACS	5.400	05/01/91		6.50	LEFANT
10	NEW YORK ST HSG FIN AGY	ST UNIV	4.700	11/01/91		6.30	RunnLtd
15	NEW YORK ST HSG FIN AGY	NON PROFIT	5.400	11/01/97		7.25	FirstCont
75	NEW YORK ST HSG FIN AGY	NON-PROF	6.400	11/01/97		6.75	FirstCont
10	NEW YORK ST HSG FIN AGY	H -N	5.200	11/01/98		7.15	Overland
10	NEW YORK ST HSG FIN AGY	URBAN	5.750	11/01/98		7.00	StoneFor
5	NEW YORK ST HSG FIN AGY	NON PROFIT	5.800	11/01/98		7.25	StoneFor
15	NEW YORK ST HSG FIN AGY	STATE UNIV	6.400	11/01/98		7.00	MidOcean
+ 15	NEW YORK ST HSG FIN AGY		7.375	11/01/98		7.20	StoneFor
100	NEW YORK ST HSG FIN AGY		7.500	11/01/98		7.00	StoneFor
500	NEW YORK ST HSG FIN AGY HOSP & NURSING HOME PROJ	*B/B*	5.400	11/01/99		7.00	BeddPill
200	NEW YORK ST HSG FIN AGY	HOSP&NURSE	5.400	11/01/99		6.90	GiantReC
10	NEW YORK ST HSG FIN AGY	*B/B* HLTH	5.600	05/01/00		7.00	GiantReC
70	NEW YORK ST HSG FIN AGY	ST UNIV	5.800	05/01/00		7.00	Overland
150	NEW YORK ST HSG FIN AGY	*B/B* ST.U	6.000	05/01/00	#	7.10	GulickCo
15	NEW YORK ST HSG FIN AGY	GEN HSG	3.750	11/01/00		100	ReidWrig
25	NEW YORK ST HSG FIN AGY	STATE UNIV	5.800	11/01/00		7.00	ReidWrig
50	NEW YORK ST HSG FIN AGY (Y/M 7.13)	P/C @ 100	7.700	11/01/00 C99	#	7.10	MidOcean
105	NEW YORK ST HSG FIN AGY HOSP & NURSING HOME PROJ		5.900	11/01/01		7.10	StoneFor
	PRUBANY PAINEWNR						
10	NEW YORK ST HSG FIN AGY	GEN HSG	4.000	11/01/02		98	StoneFor
50	NEW YORK ST PWR AUTH REV		5.900	01/01/92	#	6.30	SigmoTop
25	NEW YORK ST PWR AUTH REV		7.800	01/01/93		6.35	StoneFor

Amount	Description	Notation	Coupon	Maturity		Price	Dealer
100	NEW YORK ST PWR AUTH REV		7.250	01/01/94	#	6.60	StoneFor
200	NEW YORK ST PWR AUTH REV	*B/B*	6.750	01/01/12		97½	Gulick
55	NEW YORK ST PWR AUTH REV		6.750	01/01/12		7.25	MidOcean
250	NEW YORK ST PWR AUTH REV		7.000	01/01/16		96½	StoneFor
+ 25	NEW YORK ST PWR AUTH REV		7.000	01/01/16		7.40	StoneFor
+ 90	NEW YORK ST PWR AUTH REV		7.000	01/01/16		7.40	LittleCh.
30	NEW YORK ST PWR AUTH REV		7.000	01/01/16		7.40	HudsonBn
100	NEW YORK ST PWR AUTH REV		8.000	01/01/17		104	AlbanySec
10	NEW YORK ST PWR AUTH REV	P/R @ 103	9.750	01/01/17 C94		6.65	AlbanySec
300	NEW YORK ST PWR AUTH REV (P/R @ 103)	*REG*	9.750	01/01/17 C94		6.70	Overland
250	NEW YORK ST PWR AUTH REV		7.375	01/01/18		98½	GiantReC
+ 100	NEW YORK ST PWR AUTH REV		7.375	01/01/18		98	GiantReC
275	NEW YORK ST PWR AUTH REV		7.375	01/01/18		100	GiantReC
35	NEW YORK PWR AUTH REV	*REG*	5.000	01/01/19	#	7.40	StoneFor
150	NEW YORK ST PWR AUTH REV	CA @ 103	9.875	01/01/20 C91		6.50	StoneFor
300	NEW YORK ST PWR AUTH REV	O/PUT @ 100	5.000	03/01/20 P89		6.25	StoneFor
50	NEW YORK ST TWY AUTH EMERGENCY	AMBAC	6.000	03/01/95		6.50	StoneFor
25	NEW YORK ST TWY AUTH GEN REV		2.700	07/01/94		98	Overland
50	NEW YORK ST TWY AUTH GEN REV		2.700	07/01/94		98	Overland
50	NEW YORK ST TWY AUTH GEN REV		3.100	07/01/94		93	DowneDTv
25	NEW YORK ST TWY AUTH GEN REV		3.100	07/01/94 C		94	DowneDTv

+ Items so marked did not appear in the previous issue of The Blue List.
# Prices so marked are changed from the previous issue.
c Items so marked are reported to have call or option features. Consult offering house for full details.

Source: Adapted from *The Blue List of Current Municipal and Corporate Offerings.* The Blue List Publishing Company, a division of Standard & Poor's Corp., McGraw-Hill Financial Services Company.

Remember that The Blue List is advertising bonds that are available for sale along with who is offering those bonds. Many subscribers use The Blue List to maintain other sources in order to obtain particular state's municipal issues.

In order to correctly read The Blue List, you must understand what each column is telling you. I have taken an example and broken it into the seven columns with an explanation of what each notation means:

Amount	Security	Purpose	Rate	Maturity	Yield or Price	Offered by
$25,000	New York State HSG Fin Agy	St Univ	7.300	05/01/97	6.70	First Con
↑	↑	↑	↑	↑	↑	↑
Issue Amount	Issuer	State University	Coupon Rate	May/1/1997 Maturity Date	Yield to Maturity	Firm Offering

Once you learn to read The Blue List, you can be assured of timely and accurate information as you begin your municipal trades. Figure 8.1 provides a sample of The Blue List.

SUMMARY

To be a successful municipal securities trader, you must be cognizant and conversant in all the aspects outlined in this chapter. To review, the trader must ask himself:

Who is my audience?

What are their interests?

What is currently in the works that can affect that interest (e.g., tax law changes)?

What is the salability of this bond product?

How does it relate to other muni products?

How does it relate to other debt products?

Has the risk been correctly assessed? (If a trader disagrees with this aspect of the equation, he may take opposing trading action or shy away from the issue altogether.)

How does this type of debt compare with the same type of debt issued by another state? How does that issue trade against other types of issues from that state?

How are treasury and corporate yield curves doing as compared to munis and why?

And, of course, what is happening to interest rates; which way are they heading?

Armed with an understanding of the above-listed items and a "line of money" from the firm, the trader begins to position issues. Based on his perception of all of the above-listed items, the trader may go long, short, or stay flat. Due to the limited size of most municipal offerings, shorting issues are difficult as the ability to buy them back (to cover the short) may be limited. If the trader is not careful which instrument is chosen, the ability to buy back may be nonexistent at that time.

Chapter 9

Mortgage-Backed Securities Traders

The product that we now refer to as mortgage-backed securities had its genesis in early 1970. The Government National Mortgage Association (GNMA, also called Ginnie Mae), which had been offering debt instruments in the standard format (i.e., paid interest every 6 months and principal at maturity) brought to market a new form of instrument known as the *modified pass-through.* The product offered investors the ability to receive interest payments on the outstanding obligation and had a portion of the principal returned on a monthly basis. This was a new innovation which became the platform from which other forms of securities came to market.

As with the other forms of debt instruments, mortgage-backed securities are interest-rate sensitive. As interest rates rise, their market value falls, their yields rise, and vice versa. Unlike most other forms of debt instruments, the actual maturity date of the instrument may never be reached. Understanding this concept is what separates the mortgage-backed securities trader from other debt traders. To understand this concept, let us look at the instrument itself. We will be looking at a specialized form of the instrument known as *securitized debt*. These are issued in the form of the Ginnie Mae (Government National Mortgage Association or GNMA), the Fannie Mae (Federal National Mortgage Association or FNMA), Freddie Macs (Federal Home Loan Mortgage Corp. or FHLMC), the Sallie Mae (Student Loan Marketing Association or SLMA), as well as commercial banks and certain brokerage firms.

THE SECURITIZED MORTGAGE: THE BASIS FOR ALL MBSs

A GNMA modified pass-through, a Freddie Mac CMO, and an FNMA's REMIC are all securitized mortgages. The term *securitized mortgage* can be translated to mean securities issued against mortgages. What actually occurs is that mortgages are pooled and placed in escrow and against this, securities (i.e., certificates) are issued. Each pool is unique and the mortgages contained therein are *nonreplaceable*. This means that when a debt is paid off, it cannot be or is not replaced by a newer debt.

Let's assume "we" were involved with building 100 homes that cost $100,000 each. Based on the going conditions, the maximum 25-year mortgage on a house is $80,000 and the "average" mortgage (loan) for the 100 homes was $75,000 ($100 \times \$75,000 = \$7,500,000$). We pool the $7,500,000 worth of 25-year mortgages and issue (sell) securities representing or collateralized by the mortgages.

Two years later, a homeowner sells a home. The buyer of the 2-year-old house applies for, and receives, a new 25-year mortgage. The money borrowed by the new buyer is used to pay the seller, who in turn pays off, or retires, the original mortgage. Our pool is now reduced by one mortgage, as the new mortgage will not become part of the established pool but will either be sold, be held by the lending bank, or become part of a new pool.

If any of the remaining homeowners should refinance their homes, for example, their new mortgage would "pay off" their old mortgage, and the value of the mortgages in the pool are again reduced. Therefore, a question begs to be asked: What is the possibility that all 100 original homeowners will still be living in their homes and have their original mortgages 10 years later, 15 years later, or even 25 years later? Keep in mind, while developing your answer, that homes are not only sold when people get new job assignments in other geographical locations, but people sell their homes to buy bigger or smaller homes or buy condominiums. They refinance their mortgages when interest rates are more favorable. They sell to take advantage of tax benefits or when large bills such as a child's education must be paid. There must be 101 reasons why the 25-year mortgage will not be outstanding 25 years from inception.

From the mortgage-backed securities investors' standpoint, they are receiving monthly payments of interest plus the fact that as the homeowners make each monthly payment, a portion of that payment is used to reduce the amount of the loan and passes through to the lender. Therefore, should any of the original mortgages still be outstanding, the amount of the mortgage being received at maturity is miniscule compared to the original investment. Again, as stated earlier in this section, these instruments are not the same as regular bonds which pay back the full principal (or amount of loan) at maturity. These products actually self-deplete.

Because of this self-depleting aspect, individuals who are involved with these instruments use a term known as average life in computing yield to maturity for mortgage-backed securities. In the case of 25-year mortgages, the average life is said to be 12 to 15 years.

FACTORS AFFECTING A MORTGAGE POOL

Relocation

A particular *pool* of mortgages can be affected by many independent forces. The first factor is the geographical location of the real estate supporting the loan. The population of some areas of the country are more transient in nature than others, as the homeowners are employed in industries that rotate or reassign the personnel to different locales on a periodic basis. These individuals buy and sell their homes with some degree of regularity, living in one place for 3 to 8 years, then moving to another locale for the same period of time. Pools containing mortgages from these areas will pay down faster than pools of mortgages in other areas.

Interest Rates

The second factor facing the longevity of mortgages is the relationship of the mortgage's interest rate and the current mortgage interest or "going" interest rates. As interest rates rise, homeowners slow down in the refinancing of their homes as well as curtail purchases of new or other homes. Therefore, early payment or prepayment of mortgages slows. As interest rates fall, the reverse happens; early payment of mortgages increases. The effect of market rates on outstanding mortgages has a direct effect on the length of time the mortgages in general will be outstanding. This, in turn, changes the expected final payment date of the pool of mortgages.

Traders follow interest-rate trends and locale distributions in the trading of mortgage-backed instruments. Interest-rate trends are important, because they are the leading indicators of where the mortgage "turn over" rate will be 6 or 9 months from now. The trend is also indicative of which way mortgage rates are heading. Rising trends indicate a slow down in home turnover and a slow down in "first" home purchases. However, some people will still be buying homes, even at these "higher" rates. As rates fall from these higher levels, this pent-up demand is let loose causing a flood of new mortgages to come to market. It is a three-pronged attack:

1. Those who couldn't afford to buy a house at the higher interest level.

2. Those who had postponed moving from one home to another due to the higher rates.

3. Those who bought homes at higher rates and will now refinance the mortgages at lower rates.

One of the interesting aspects of this product is the direct involvement of people. It is one of the few products that have individuals participating on both sides of the market. Individuals buy homes by taking out mortgages; on the other side, individuals buy the mortgages as an investment. It is very possible that a homeowner with a mortgage may also own Ginnie Maes or Freddie Macs in his portfolio of securities investments.

The Problems with Cash Flow

To the individual investor, the value of a dollar is not a dollar. It is perceived value at a given point in time. For example, an individual's cash can fall into two categories: cash flow and savings. *Cash flow* is what an individual exists on from payday to payday. *Savings* is accumulated cash lying idle, hopefully earning interest. When mortgages are issued, they usually contain a prepayment penalty clause for the first few years.

As mortgage rates fall, individuals realize that they could increase their cash flow by refinancing their mortgages at a lower rate. Their dollars in the savings account now appear to be worth less than the dollars in their cash flow, so they pay the penalty and refinance. This course of action has a direct effect on the expected life of newer mortgages. If a trader believes that the prepayment penalty is a deterrent and the homeowners do not, the trader will make a very bad error in calculating the value of the instrument. The trader will calculate the yield to maturity over a longer period of time and would be selling the instruments at prices below their true or actual value.

TRADING MORTGAGE-BACKED
SECURITY PRODUCTS

Traders involved with Ginnie Maes (GNMAs) usually trade several forms of the product. There are *TBAs, forwards, standbys,* and *calls.*

Trading TBAs

TBAs (or *To Be Announced*) securities are originated by mortgage bankers and sold to Ginnie Mae (GNMA) dealers. *Mortgage bankers* are entities which arrange for the financing of mortgages in certain areas of the country. One of their functions entails obtaining funds from money-dense areas of the country, like New England, for use in money-sparse areas, such as the Southwest. For the most part, mortgage bankers are not banks, but subsidiaries of construction companies and the like.

Individuals needing mortgages in these regions use the services of the mortgage banker. Some of these prospective home buyers will qualify for VA (Veterans Administration), FHA (Federal Housing Authority), or FmHA (Farmers Home Administration) loans. Others will not qualify for government backing and these will become conventional mortgages. Some of these mortgages will be pooled and sold, while others will be sold as is.

Mortgage bankers have potential risk in working toward the financing of mortgages. There is a time delay between when mortgages are approved and when they are in force. Should interest rates change from the time the mortgage is approved to the time it is in force, the mortgage banker could face a loss when selling the newly enforced mortgage in the marketplace.

In the case of Ginnie Maes (GNMAs), the mortgage bankers sell these pooled, government-approved, but not enforced, mortgages known as TBAs to Ginnie Mae dealers (traders). These transactions have a defined quantity coupon rate, maturity date, as well as all other aspects of a debt instrument. What is missing is the unique pool number that is assigned by the GNMA which identifies the pool of mortgages.

Since a TBA represents a pool of approved, but not enforced, government-backed mortgages, the only part of complete pool description that is missing is the unique pool number which will be assigned by the GNMA when all mortgages are in place. The mortgage banker will sell this TBA to the Ginnie Mae dealer that is willing to pay the highest price. The Ginnie Mae dealer, in turn, trades these instruments against other firms and/or customers.

TBAs are noninterest bearing instruments that trade at full-contract value. The duration is established at the time of trade, and delivery must be made by the seller to the buyer as required by the TBA contract. As the contract stipulates, the rate of interest to be delivered is fixed or set and the price of the instrument can fluctuate as interest rates change in the marketplace during the life of the TBA.

Ginnie Mae dealers usually have several TBA positions working at one time. They buy and sell TBAs and price them by their interest rates as well as by the different delivery months. The trader tries to profit by:

1. Buying and selling via their quote spread in a given delivery month. By acquiring the position at the bid and selling at their offer they earn a profit on the turnaround.

2. "Playing" one month delivery against another month, or trying to obtain an interest-rate spread, one against the other.

3. Maintaining an overall long or short position.

Buying and selling off their quote is the same in this product as it is in any product. The traders attempt to buy at prices (bid) which are lower than the prices at which they are willing, or hoping, to sell (offer). Sometimes, if interest rates appear to be rising, prices are falling, the traders may sell first then buy back at a lower price. As in other products, this is not a guaranteed method of making a profit as competing traders at other firms could be making a "better" market. Values, in general, could change while the trader is "holding" either the long or short position. (Remember, it takes two parties to make a trade.)

Some traders take advantage of interest-rate spreads between expiring TBAs. There is an increasing risk factor in this as a TBA "goes out" for longer periods of time. The longer the exposure to market, the greater the risk. The risk is compensated for by the price of the TBA. For example:

1. At the present time, a $9\frac{1}{2}\%$ mortgage is worth a $1 for a $1 of loan. What would you pay for the mortgage pool that would pay interest immediately?

2. What would you pay for a pool of $9\frac{1}{2}\%$ mortgages that are coming to market and will begin to pay interest 2 months from now?

3. What would you pay for a pool of 9 ½% mortgages that are coming to market and will begin to pay interest 4 months from now?

If you believe that all three examples should have the same $1 for $1 of debt cost, then you are saying interest rates will be 100% flat (unchanged) for the next 4 months. Is that realistic? Wouldn't you want some protection for buying the 4-month TBA over the 2-month TBA? Remember, if interest rates rise, the value of the 9 ½% TBAs will fall. The individual who purchased the current pool is getting a return on the investment. The individual who purchased the 2-month TBA has a commitment to pay par ($1 for $1) regardless of what the TBAs are really worth 2 months from now. Finally, the individual who purchased the 4-month TBA is committed to pay par ($1 for $1) regardless of what the TBAs are worth.

For the 2- or 4-month commitment, the buyer is entitled to a "break" or discount for the risk. Therefore, in usual situations, the greater the risk, the lower the price.

Traders have a "feeling" of what is fair compensation for this risk. If they perceive that the market has overcompensated for the risk, they will sell the nearer-term TBA and purchase the farther out-term TBA. If they are correct, the "gap" between the two should narrow as time passes. Therefore, later on they will reverse the position, buying in what they sold and selling what they bought.

Example: The following is a list of how TBAs could trade over a 2-month period:

Current outstanding 9 ½ mortgages = $1 profit for $1 of debt.

2-month TBAs (9 ½%) currently trading at 98¢ for $1 of debt.

4-month TBAs (9 ½%) currently trading at 95¢ per $1 of debt.

Sell 2 mo. TBA @ 98.

Buy 4 mo. TBA @ 95.

2 months pass and interest rates have not changed.

What *was* a 2-month TBA *is* now coming to market $1 for $1 of debt.

What *was* a 4-month TBA *is* now a 2-month TBA 98¢ for $1 of debt.

Buy current TBA @ $1 for two-point loss.

Sell 2-month TBA @ 98¢ for three-point profit. Net profit = 1 point.

If, however, the trader believed that the spread was not enough, then the reverse position would be taken.

TBAs and Hedging. In the previous examples, a form of protection known as *hedging* was brought into play. The positions taken offered some protection if the trader was incorrect. The losses on one side would be partially or totally offset by the profits on the other side. The trader was in fact "playing" the spread (basis point spread) between two different TBAs. If, theoretically, the spread remained constant, it wouldn't matter if interest rates rose or fell during the position period, as the trader would close the position at the same spread rate under which the position was opened.

Example: A 2-month TBA is trading at 96, a 4-month TBA is trading at 95 which equals a one-point spread. Interest rates rise and the 2-month TBA is now trading at 95 ½, the 4-month TBA is trading at 94 ½ which is equal to a one-point spread. Therefore, even though the movement of interest rates changed, the value of the TBAs, its effect on both positions was the same.

TBA traders who have a belief in the movements' interest rates will take and maintain positions based on that belief. Remember, TBAs are paid for when they settle (i.e., a 2-month TBA bought today, must be paid for when it comes due 2 months from now), whereas the sale of such an instrument requires the delivery of an actual GNMA pool at the end of the 2-month period.

Let's assume that a trader believes mortgage rates are on the rise. Therefore, the market value of TBAs will decline. The trader could simply sell (short) the position and do nothing until the movement of mortgage rates proved the decision correct or incorrect. The trader could also trade from a short position, meaning that they are buying and selling against the quotes but maintaining an overall short position all the time.

The advantage to the trader is twofold. One, there is an opportunity to profit from trading the quote spread; and two, as the overall position is short a profit is realized when the value in the marketplace falls. For example, the traders market for a given TBA listed at 98 ¼ would be:

Sell (short) $10,000,000 at 98 ¼;

Bid 98 ⅛ for $5,000,000;

Quote now at 98 ⅛–¼;

Buy $5,000,000 @ 98 ⅛;

Offer $5,000,000 @ 98 ³⁄₁₆;

Quote now at 98 ⅛–³⁄₁₆;

Drop the bid to 98 making the quote 98-³⁄₁₆;

If the trader cannot find a buyer at 98 ³⁄₁₆, lower the offer to 98 ⅛ and try to sell the $5,000,000 at the same price that it was purchased at or try to buy more at 98, knowing it would lower the overall position price allowing the TBA to be reoffered at ¹⁄₁₆, ³⁄₃₂, ⅛, ⁵⁄₃₂, or ³⁄₁₆.

The trader's objective in the above scenario is to profit from trading in a declining market. Not every trade will be profitable and the trader must realize this. It is the overall objective that must be met; the greater the success in achieving it, the sweeter the reward. Naturally, if the trader believed mortgage rates were going to drop, the trader would maintain and trade out of a long position.

Three Types of Orders for TBA Trading. An interesting aspect of mortgage-backed securities trading is that each pool of mortgages develops its own characteristics. Some pools can be more attractive than others of the same coupon rate and approximate maturity date. Therefore, traders use three types of orders in transacting business in these products. They are:

1. Known pool;

2. Guaranteed coupon transactions; and

3. Yield maintenance.

A trader selling a known pool is stipulating the exact pool of mortgages by the number being sold at the time of trade. The seller in this trade must be able to deliver that specific pool.

Example: A trader from Stone, Forrest, and River buys $10,000,000 GNMA 9% Pool #31313X @ 98 from Giant Reckor, and Crane. When Giant Reckor, and Crane delivers the issue in settlement of the trade, the pool number must be 31313X. A delivery of any other 9% pool would not be good delivery.

Guaranteed coupon transactions state that any pool of mortgages, up to three different pools per million, can be delivered against a transaction as long as the coupon rate of the pool is the same as that which is called for in the transaction. Due to the fact that instruments such as GNMAs pay principal and interest monthly, the amount of principal outstanding decreases month by month. As stated earlier, unlike the standard form of bonds which pay off all of the principal borrowed at maturity, these instruments self-deplete. It is, therefore, almost impossible to satisfy the exact contracted dollar amount called for in the transaction. For example, the buyer of a $1,000,000 GNMA pool will *not* receive $1,000,000 of principal at delivery. The mortgages comprising the pool are being paid down by the homeowners. To accommodate this feature, a "fudge factor" or tolerance level is brought into play. At the present time, up to three different pools can be delivered per million as long as their total principal is not over or under 2.4999% of the million dollar contract and no two pools satisfy the "under 2.4999%" portion of the tolerance level.

Example: A trade of $1,000,000 GNMA 9½% takes place between Stone, Forrest, and Rivers (SF&R) and Giant Reckor, and

Crane (GR&C). The selling firm can deliver up to three pools to satisfy the transaction. The total principal of the delivery can range from $1,024,000.00 to $975,000.01 with no two pools adding up to the $975,000.01 figures.

As a trader, it is important to remember this point. If interest rates have risen between the trade and settlement dates, the delivery firm will try to overdeliver, thereby capturing as many higher dollars as possible. If, however, interest rates have fallen, the deliverers will try to underdeliver.

Example: Let's say the price at the time the contract for trade was made is 98¢ per $1. The value of the pools at the time of delivery is 99¢ per $1. The pools in the inventory are:

Pool	Principal
13622X	$343,855.50
14293X	$489,429.80
15881X	$185,829.50
16234X	$141,715.00

As interest rates have fallen and the value of the pools has risen, the deliverer would try to deliver the minimum dollar of principal required so as to maximize the profit or value remaining in the portfolio. The deliverer would, therefore, deliver Pools 13622X, 14293X, and 16234X for a total principal of $975,000.30 thus leaving Pool 15881X in inventory, which has increased in value $18,582.95 from the time of the trade (99¢ − 98¢ = .01¢ × $185,829.50 = $18,582.95).

If, however, the price had fallen from 98¢ to 97¢, the deliverer would have used pool 15881X instead of pool 16234X thereby minimizing the loss of the portfolio to $14,171.50 (98¢ − 97¢ = .01¢ × $141,715.00 = $14,171.50).

The last method of trading is used when interest rates are highly volatile. It is known as *yield maintenance.* The seller may deliver any coupon GNMA as long as it is priced to yield what the contracted pool GNMA is yielding.

Example: Stone, Forrest, and Rivers buys $1,000,000 GNMAs priced to yield what a 9 1/2% is currently yielding from Giant

Reckor, and Crane. GR&C can deliver any coupon GNMA as long as it is priced to yield what a 9 1/2% GNMA is yielding at the time of trade. As you can note from the following example bid quote, the higher the coupon rate the higher the yield. In order to have a higher coupon instrument yield what a lower coupon instrument is yielding, the price would have to be raised.

An example bid quote would be

8 1/2% GNMA Bid 94 26/32 YTM 9.23

9% GNMA Bid 97 14/32 YTM 9.48

A *yield maintenance transaction* based on an 8 1/2% GNMA, but being settled with a 9% GNMA would necessitate raising the price of the 9% to over par in order to get the 9.23 yield to maturity required in the settlement of the trade. Remember, as interest rates fall, *debt prices rise,* and in turn, *yields fall.* The price at delivery would have to be increased (meaning, buying over par) in order to get the yield down to 9.23.

In trading on a yield maintenance basis, care must be taken to initiate safeguards in the settlement of the transaction. For example, a yield maintenance transaction should be consummated with a coupon rate which is trading close to par (or the face amount of the issue). The buyer may include the phrase *par cap* within his trade negotiations. This means that regardless of the coupon rate, the buyer will pay current market value or par (face value), whichever is less. The buyer would negotiate a yield maintenance contract near par with a par cap in order to limit the exposure.

Trading Forwards

The vast majority of mortgage-backed securities transactions settle once a month on a specified date. Trades executed after that date will settle the following month. Due to these delayed delivery procedures, these transactions are known as *forwards.* A forward is defined as a contract traded over the counter in which one party guarantees to deliver a specified instrument at a future date, in return for which the other party guarantees a set price. Each forward is a negotiated contract.

A forward can be, and usually is, specified for 1 month, although the time limitation can be longer. Also, because of the trading similarities between TBAs and forwards, many traders use the terms interchangeably. They are so similar that at the time of delivery, the operations personnel do not differentiate between the two types of instruments. But, for the record, TBAs are initially offered by mortgage bankers against new issues. Forwards are traded between industry participants and represent outstanding pools which have not been identified at the time of trade.

Trading Standbys and Calls

Trading in mortgage-backed securities includes trading *standbys* and *calls*. These optionlike instruments are negotiated between parties and give the owner the privilege to sell (standby) or buy (call) a prestated quantity of a certain GNMA coupon rate issue at a predetermined price for a finite period of time. For this privilege, the buyer pays the seller a premium. Unlike other forms of options that we are familiar with, these products are not standardized and trade over the counter.

In some firms, the standby is "booked" as a sell when it is purchased and, therefore, it is booked as a buy when it is sold. The reason for this abnormality is that standbys are booked by what the standby does, not by its position. Calls are booked in the usual manner, buys for buys, and sells as sells.

Standbys were the first of these two products to be offered. They were originally used to hedge GNMA positions. Standbys gave (and still give) the GNMA owner the opportunity to sell GNMAs under this negotiated contract, should the GNMA holder so desire. If the GNMA holder did not want to exercise this privilege, the contract would expire. To make the standby contract a better trading vehicle and in order to bring liquidity to that marketplace, there was a need for a vehicle that would give its owner the privilege of buying. Therefore, calls were introduced. Certain traders now specialize and trade in standbys and calls only.

Standbys and calls are traded in a similar fashion to regular options. Against a TBA or forward contract position, a firm, say

Giant Reckor, and Crane (GR&C), "sells" standbys to Stone, Forrest, and Rivers (SF&R). These standbys set a price at which GR&C can sell the instruments to SF&R if they so desire.

Example: With GNMA 9 1/2% trading at 96, GR&C "sells" $10,000,000 9 1/2% standbys with a strike price of 96 to SF&R for one-half point. SF&R is now obligated to buy $10MM (1,000,000 = 1MM) @ 96 on a specific date should GR&C want to sell. For accepting this obligation, SF&R will be paid one-half point ($5,000 per million dollars of principal) the next business day.

Assuming that GR&C acquired the GNMA position @ 96, the break-even point now becomes 96 1/2. As SF&R received one-half point payment, should they have to acquire the $10MM worth of GNMA @ 96, their break-even point is 95 1/2.

Looking at this position from GR&C's viewpoint, they own $10MM of 9 1/2% GNMA forwards or TBAs at a total cost of 96 1/2. If they are able to sell the position later at a price above 96 1/2, they will have a profit. If they sell the position at a price ranging down from 96 1/2 to 96, they will be left with a break-even point of 96 1/2 to a maximum one-half point loss of 96 (i.e., bought @ 96 1/2, sold @ 96). If the position is worth less than 96, GR&C will still only lose one-half of a point, as they would deliver the instruments versus the payment of 96 to SF&R.

From the viewpoint of SF&R, they will receive $5,000 per million × 10 = $50,000 cash the next business day. The underlying issue is at 96 and SF&R's break-even is 95 1/2. SF&R's traders could do the following:

1. Nothing.

2. Try to "sell" the standbys to someone else for less than one-half point, thereby locking in the difference in a premium spread.

3. Short the 9 1/2% TBAs or forwards and buy calls at 96 for less than one-half point. This position would render price movements neutral and would concentrate on premium moves.

4. Trade a different month's standby against the position.

In other words, SF&R traders have many different strategies that they can employ. It is a full-scale trading operation. The decision as to which strategies to employ is based, of course, on the individual's perception of the market. However, as this is a customized set of contracts, the traders' ability to be profitable also must include the ability to successfully negotiate a contract. In this segment of the marketplace, the difference between a profit or loss can be determined by $1/32$ or even $1/64$ of a point. Remember, a round lot in these instruments is $1 million; $1/64$ of a point then becomes $156.25.

For any product to be successful, it must have multiple trading capabilities. The more applicable a product is to different situations, the better it would be as a trading vehicle. This is also true for products like standbys.

The fact that the product was originated in order to assist GNMA dealers in hedging their positions is true, but what about the seller of the standby. Besides receiving a premium the next business day from the GNMA hedger, the seller of the standby must be able to trade against that position.

The standby trader could short a TBA or forward expecting the price to drop. If the standby trader is correct, the GNMA hedger will exercise the standby at the contracted price, closing out the standby trader's short position. Here's a list of steps describing how this procedure works:

1. The standby trader sells $1MM standby to a GNMA trader on 9% GNMAs expiring in 6 months at a price of $96 and receives a premium of one-half point.

2. The standby trader then sells 1MM TBA 9% for delivery in 6 months at 96.

3. Interest rates rise and the value of 9% GNMAs falls.

4. The GNMA trader exercises standby against the standby trader at a price of 96, who in turn delivers it against the short sale.

In this strategy, if the market price should rise, the standby trader is at risk since the GNMA trader will not exercise the standby if he can get a better price in the market. The standby trader would have to buy into the "short" GNMA position at a possible loss.

The standby trader could try to find someone else to purchase a standby from (preferably with the same terms but at a lower price than the one the standby trader just sold). If this could be done, the standby trader would have a locked-in profit (having sold it for more than it was acquired for) with no exposure.

A standby gives the owner the privilege of selling; the seller of the standby must wait to see what the standby's owner may or may not do. The standby concept and the marketplace could be greatly enhanced if an instrument existed that could give its owner the privilege to buy. Calls were introduced because of this need. A call is defined as a feature by which all or part of an issue may be redeemed before maturity and under certain specified conditions.

A standby trader could now have the ability to *call in* (buy) GNMAs against preestablished contracts as well as being forced to receive them by the standby owner. The standby trader can now better control his trading position through the use of owning or selling standbys and calls.

Trading Repos and Reverse Repos

Used primarily as a form of financing, *repos* (repurchase agreements) are contracts entered into between the owner of the mortgage-backed security (usually the trading firm) and an institution that has noninvestable funds. The most common form of this is the *overnight repo*. Under this concept, the trading firm "sells" the security for cash (same trade and settlement dates) and agrees to "repurchase" it for tomorrow's settlement. The difference between the price of the sale and the repurchase is the interest paid by the seller to the buyer for the use of the money.

Example: Stone, Forrest, and Rivers (SF&R) must finance a $25 million GNMA which they are maintaining "overnight." SF&R has paid the seller and arranges for funding. SF&R can pledge the security at a bank and pay a brokers call rate (the rate banks charge broker dealers for collateralized loans). While SF&R "owns" the issue they will receive interest; but as they must borrow money to carry the position, they also must pay interest. The difference between what interest is received and what is paid can be a profit, known as *positive cost of carry,* or a loss, known as *negative cost of carry.*

As the amount of interest received is set by the instrument, the amount paid offers the trader an opportunity to earn profits. The lower the rate of interest paid by the firm on borrowed funds, the greater the opportunity for profit.

As SF&R was eager to get into the repo, the lending institution is equally eager to lend the money. SF&R will then enter into a repo with the lending institution. The lending institution is entering into *reverse repo* (buying first then reselling the issue back to SF&R at an agreed to price). The difference between what the value of the repo/reverse repo is when it is established and the price at which it is closed out at represents the interest paid on the loan.

The Match Book. Firms that have large repo operations get involved with an interesting trading mechanism known as the *match book*. Under this process, repo traders try to "pair off" reverse repos and repos trying to profit from the difference in interest rates.

Example: The firm of LaSalle & Marquette needs to finance 50MM ($50 million) worth of GNMAs overnight. They do not have access to a lending institution. They call Stone, Forrest, and Rivers' "repo desk" and ask if there is interest in doing a repo. The repo manager calls some contacts and "lines up" $50 million with Riviera Consolidated, Inc. The rate to be paid on the $50 million is 6 1/2%. SF&R's repo manager then gets back on the phone with LaSalle & Marquette and offers the financing at 6 3/4%. The manager of LaSalle accepts.

LaSalle & Marquette		*SF&R*		*Riviera Cons., Inc.*
Repo 6 3/4%	$\longrightarrow$	Reverse Repo		
		Repo 6 1/2%	$\longrightarrow$	Reverse Repo

If all goes smoothly, the two repos will unwind and SF&R will be left with a profit of 1/4% on $50 million.

The concept of the match book is to maintain offsetting entries of reverse repos versus repos with the firm earning revenue from the difference between the interest being received (reverse repo) and the interest being paid (repo). The repo traders would never let the two parties speak to each other because that would neutralize SF&R's worth.

The risks involved in "running" a match book include the dangers of one participant becoming insolvent or of one party needing its part of the investment returned (securities/cash) ahead of time, thereby leaving one "leg" of the match book open. SF&R's repo manager may choose to maintain a loss position rather than calling off the remaining "leg" as this would get the client very annoyed at SF&R.

Open and Closed Repos. Repos may also be open or closed. A *closed repo* has its interest rate and maturity date set at the time the contract is entered into. An *open repo* may have either the interest rate or close-out date, or both, not set. The interest rate in an open-end repo is negotiated and based off some other rate such as federal funds or T Bills. The ability of the repo manager to get the most favorable rate is key to the overall financial success of the company.

Contacts and the Successful Repo Trader. The most important asset a repo manager or repo trader has is contacts. The ability to raise the most money for the lowest rate is of paramount importance. It is through this vehicle that the repo manager (trader) can successfully finance the firm's Treasury, agency, and certain money markets instruments as well as "run" a profitable match book.

PASS-THROUGHS VERSUS COLLATERALIZED MORTGAGE OBLIGATIONS (CMOs)

The instrument that we have been concentrating on so far in this chapter is the GNMA modified pass-through. Another form of pooled mortgages is known as *CMOs* or *collateralized mortgage obligations*. The primary difference between these forms of mortgages is twofold.

In modified pass-throughs, principal is "passed" through to the debt owners in proportion to the quantity owned. No debt owner would be paid off ahead of any other owner of the same pool. To keep track of the amount of principal still outstanding in a given pool, the industry uses *factor tables* which are issued on a monthly basis. You would obtain the current principal by multiplying the current factor presented on the factor table by the original value of the pool.

Example: Let us assume you purchased $1,003,855.20 worth of a pool. Five years have gone by, during which time you have been receiving interest and principal on a monthly basis. Now you want to know how much principal is still remaining. To determine this you could:

Add up all the principal payments that you received (12 months × 5 years = 60), all 60 of them!

Or simply check this month's factor tables. Locate your pool number and then multiply your pool's original value by the factor. Assume this month's factor for your pool is .7273110. $1,003,855.20 × .7273110 = $730,114.92. This means that over the 5-year period, you've received $273,740.30 in principal payments.

Conversely, under CMOs, the principal payments are directed to a time-sequenced prepayment schedule. The schedules contain levels that are known as *tranches* or *layers*. The first tranche must get paid before the second, and so on. A tranche can be paid off before the due date, but not after.

In trading CMOs, two factors affect pricing methodology: the prepayment applications from the modified pass-through and the time in force. A short-term tranche should be priced as an intermediate instrument and not a long-term investment. Also, by tracking the payoff history of the issues' early tranches, one can make assumptions about the payment habits of longer-term ones.

In trading the pass-through, the trader must be concerned with the payback of principal for the entire instrument. In the case of CMOs, each tranche covers a different time span so they must trade as such. For example, the accurate perception of what interest rates will be at a number of given points in time plays a critical part in the pricing decision.

Let's look at 25-year mortgages and compare pass-throughs versus CMOs for five tranches:

Years	Interest Rate Changes
1– 5	Interest rates rise
5–10	Interest rates unchanged
10–15	Interest rates fall
15–20	Interest rates rise
20–25	Interest rates remain unchanged

Years 1 through 5 would result in a slower than expected prepayment schedule for pass-throughs as cost of relocation becomes increasingly expensive. In one case, with the CMO, the first tranche (assume 5 years) will be paid off by its due date.

Years 5 through 10 pass-throughs would see an increase in prepayments as people would tend to get used to the rates and accept the extra expense. CMOs second tranche and part of the third are paid off ahead of schedule.

Years 10 to 15 would see an increase in prepayments as homeowners take advantage of falling rates. The pay-downs shorten the average life computation of the pass-through. The third tranche and most of the fourth of the CMOs are prepaid down ahead of schedule *but* the fifth tranche has not yet been prepaid at all.

In years 15 to 20, pass-through prepayment slows and begins to track the expected prepayment schedules for mortgages outstanding for 15 to 20 years. In the CMO issue, the fourth tranche is paid off ahead of schedule, and the fifth is paid off when due.

At the start of the pricing process for these two issues, the trader had to be concerned with what percentage of the principal in the pass-through would be paid back by what date. In the case of the CMO, when the third tranche, let's say, would be paid back is important, but equally important is that the owners of the third tranche would not see any principal payments until the second tranche is completely paid off.

In Figure 9.1, principal and interest is paid to *all* the pass-through holders in direct proportion to what they own. If 20% of

Figure 9.1. Pictoral Display of Pass-Through versus CMO Ownership.

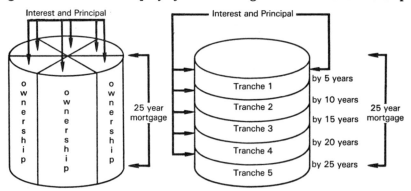

the principal has been paid down, all owners of the pass-through have received 20%. In the CMO example, interest is paid to the tranche owners but principal is paid to each tranche in order of maturity. In Figure 9.1 each 5 years represented 20% of the entire CMO, so 20% has been paid back. Tranche 1 would have been paid off with tranche 2 through 5 receiving nothing.

The first instrument of the group to break the standard bond mold was the GNMA with its modified pass-through. Instead of receiving interest every 6 months and principal at the end of the "borrow" life, an investor could now receive interest and principal on a monthly basis. To some users that did not do all that they wanted, so the CMO was designed for them. It pays interest while curtailing the principal payment until a specified time zone. As time passes other variations will be introduced as required by the population, or due to tax changes or due to users' or issuers' needs.

SUMMARY

As a mortgage-backed securities trader, you have to make decisions as to which of the securities or types of issues to trade or make markets in. In most cases, this is dependent on the amount of funds under the trader's control. Usually, the trader will specialize in TBAs and forwards, standbys and calls, round lot, odd lot, or even seasoned or unseasoned pools.

TBA or forwards are difficult to differentiate from a trading standpoint. Both are usually delayed delivery (i.e., next month). One method to separate the two would be to determine who the seller is. If the seller is a mortgage banker, chances are it's a TBA. The duration of the delayed delivery is also indicative of the origin as TBAs usually have longer delayed delivery periods.

The term *delayed delivery* is used on a macro level for any transaction that does not settle in a 5-business-day period. As mortgage-backed securities usually settle once per month, the method of delivery is known as delayed delivery. TBAs usually settle in 4 to 6 month periods of time.

A trader who specializes in short-term forwards/TBA (next month) must be concerned with the deliverables being received against these trades. Because mortgage-backed securities pay principal and interest monthly, the tolerance level on delivery could affect the profitability of the trader. Therefore, it is important for the trader to know with whom the trades are being transacted.

For example, if most of the transactions that the trader is involved with concern participants that have portfolio or inventory positions, the trader would receive principal above par in falling markets and below par in rising markets. This is caused by the fact that participants are manning their positions to take advantage of the market movement.

In trading TBAs, some traders attempt to position one month against another when the interest spread does not appear to be in accordance with the trader's perception. The trader could buy one month, sell another, and wait for the positions to "come into line" or accept delivery against the buy transaction. In this way, the trader could collect interest and principal from the security itself and deliver it against the sell transaction when the sell transaction settles.

As the trader goes in and out of transactions, two trails are being established. (Remember, in the case of the TBAs and forwards no money changes hands until the transaction settles.) The first is a series of positions, settling in different months or hedged against other trader vehicles (i.e., TBAs versus standbys), the second in a series of (paired off) transactions (buy/sell, sell/buy) resulting in a series of profit and losses.

A mortgage-backed security trader, dealing in TBAs and forwards attempts to earn revenue from buying/selling the same monthly TBA, or by spreading one month against another and by hedging or offsetting positions by use of other instruments. Strategies will vary from trader to trader and as market conditions change from period to period.

CMO and pass-through traders are not only comparing yields against their expected time outstanding but also against other CMO and pass-through instruments trying to uncover price discrepancies that can be traded against.

In order to achieve an understanding of yields, traders must be sensitive as to where public and institutional interest lies. The more interest there is in a particular time period, the more trading activity will occur, and therefore, the more market makers will enter the trading arena. The result is tighter quotes and more liquid markets. The less interest there is in a particular segment, the fewer the market makers, the less liquidity, the wider the spread of the quotes would be, the riskier it is for a trader to maintain a position, and the more revenue the market maker can earn per trade. This is true of most, if not all, trading instruments.

Some may look at this scenario as the easier it is to make a profit, the more participants will enter the trading arena therefore creating smaller earnings. On the other hand, the harder the profit, the more participation decreases and, therefore, the greater the earnings. However, as more participants enter the marketplace and revenue per trade diminishes, so does the potential risk of loss. As less participants enter the marketplace, the revenue per transaction increases, but so does the risk of loss.

This concept usually holds true, but has within it a false sense of security. Traders unwilling to assume the risk of market exposure in less active issues will offset the limited profit potential of the more active trading issues by assuming larger than usual positions. By maintaining larger positions, the trader can trade more and thereby earn the revenue through volume. The fallacy in this concept is that a severe and adverse market move will send many of the "flat" traders scurrying away. This will leave the position trader with a trading inventory that is losing money and has no way to easily unwind (or get out of the position).

Chapter 10

International Traders

One of the major areas of growth in the U.S. marketplace is the field of foreign securities and foreign currencies. The growing interest in the foreign securities and currencies market has developed because of technical advancements in communications and the strength of these international markets. Some may say that it is also the volatility of the U.S. dollar that is the leading factor for this market's growth.

HOW TRADERS USE THE INTERNATIONAL MARKETPLACE TO GENERATE PROFITS

As stated throughout this book, a marketplace exists because of a need (demand). That need must be multifaceted, serving different purposes for different users. Some trade on the day-to-day differences within this international market. There must be other individuals, though, willing to trade on the aberrations of this marketplace.

Example: A U.S. importer has purchased merchandise from Italy and must pay for it in Italian lira. Part of the merchandise being imported will be sold in Canada and, therefore, paid for in Canadian dollars. At this moment, $100 of U.S. currency will buy 128,200 lira or $100 of U.S. currency will buy 120 Canadian dollars. The converse of this is that 100 lira will buy .08¢ U.S. and $1.00 Canada will buy .84¢ U.S.

If the dollar (U.S.) falls against the lira, you would need more dollars to buy lira. Each dollar would buy less lira, and the product would become more *expensive* to import, thereby diminishing the profit opportunity.

Would the situation be helped if the Canadian dollar rose against the U.S. dollar? Would that change help or hurt the situation?

If the Canadian dollar rose against the U.S. dollar (or the U.S. dollar fell against the Canadian dollar) you would need more U.S. dollars to buy Canadian dollars or less Canadian dollars to buy U.S. dollars. Therefore, it would help, as while it is more expensive to import, the U.S. merchant could sell his imports in Canada for more U.S. dollars because it would cost less in Canadian dollars.

Let's see if this is correct. Using the aforementioned example, and keeping everything basic: for $100 U.S. you can import a product that would sell in Italy for 128,200 lira and sell it in Canada for $120 Canadian. If all other aspects of these transactions (i.e., shipping charges) were free, the importer could at this point be breaking even.

Let's assume the dollar fell against the lira to where a dollar would only buy 124,000 lira. The product that cost 128,200 lira would now cost more than $100 U.S., making it more expensive to acquire. It would cost about $103 U.S. If the importer was working on a 5% mark up, the product would be priced domestically to sell at $105. Three dollars of a possible $5 profit would be eaten up if the selling price did not change.

In Canada, the product exported at $120 Canadian would be sold for $126 giving a 5% mark up. If the U.S. dollar fell against the Canadian dollar to where $1.00 U.S. would buy $1.10 Canadian, then in order to maintain the 5% mark up, it would be necessary to raise the price of $115.50 Canadian which is $10.50 Canadian less than it was originally intended to be sold for. Which means if $120 Canadian is a fair value, the more we can sell at $120 Canadian, the greater our profit will be. Instead of a 5% mark up, the merchandiser would be charging 9%+ mark up.

What if it cost Canadian manufacturers $120 to manufacture this product? They would see their share of their own market shrink because the imports would be less expensive. What about the marketplace in Italy? They would be exporting less to America as the lira continued to climb against the dollar.

As the lira continued to climb, the U.S. importer would start to look for merchandise from other countries, as well as looking for ways to produce the product domestically.

From the American businessperson's viewpoint, as the dollar falls against other currencies, imports get more expensive and exports get cheaper. As the dollar rises against other currencies, imports become cheaper and exports become more expensive.

In the above example, we used the U.S. dollar against the Italian lira and the Canadian dollar. However, everything does not move that simply. Let's see what was overlooked. How about the Canadian dollar against the Italian lira. In our example, both currencies moved up against the dollar. But what about against each other? At one point, $100 U.S. would buy 128,200 lira or $120 Canadian; at another point, it could buy 124,000 lira or $110 Canadian. At first, $100 Canadian would buy 106,834 lira, but then it could buy 112,727 lira. The Canadian dollar has actually risen against lira, making the Italian-made article less expensive to acquire in Canada.

CURRENCY TRADERS

Currency traders try to position themselves between the different currencies of the international market in anticipation of their moves. In the case of European currencies, there is a common currency known as *European currency units* or ECUs. ECUs are comprised of the currencies of 10 countries in different proportions.

The ECU's 10 currencies are:

the Belgian franc;

the British pound sterling;

the Danish krona;

the Dutch guilder;

the French franc;

the Greek drachma;

the Irish pound;

the Italian lira;

the Luxembourg franc; and

the West German deutche mark.

This common currency offers currency traders the ability to hedge currency position by using the ECU to offset a position. This can be done through *multicurrency positioning.* For example, a trader could buy the German mark, buy the ECU, and sell the Swiss franc. This would be done if the mark was rising against the ECU faster than the ECU was rising against the Swiss franc.

Currency Futures and Options

Currency traders also have the benefit of futures and options to offset or hedge positions. Futures set the date at which a delivery will take place in the future. Options permit the owner of the option to exercise the contract if they so desire. If they don't want to, they don't have to; it is their option. A currency trader may sell a futures contract on, let's say the British pound sterling that he may have in position. The future will guarantee the price that the British pounds could be sold at a later date, thereby minimizing the trader's risk.

Example: A trader is long in the British pound sterling market at $1.81 U.S. The British pound sterling 3-month future is at $1.75 U.S. The trader has minimized his risk to .06¢ per British pound by selling the future. If the British pound falls against the dollar, then it would take less dollars to buy the British pound sterling. Once the British pound sterling has fallen below $1.75, the trader could deliver the pounds in position against the futures at delivery time.

In similar respect, the trader could have utilized options. A currency *call* option gives the owner the privilege of buying a finite quantity of the underlying currency by a certain date at a predetermined price. A *put* option would give the owner the privilege of selling a finite quantity of underlying currency by a certain date at a fixed price. The seller of the contract, known as the *writer,* is obligated to perform the terms of the contract if an owner decides to exercise. For this privilege or option, the owner (buyer) pays the seller (writer) a premium.

A currency trader long in a particular currency can sell (write) call options against the position. This would bring in revenue, (the premium) but could limit the profit potential as the more profitable the currency position became, the more likely the currency will be *called* away by someone who owned a call. Traders in judging the proper strategies must take the risk/reward factors into the analysis process at all times. What the expected result of the currency position is would determine whether or not the trader perceives the writing of calls as a good strategy.

Sometimes foreign currency traders work with traders specializing in foreign instruments. These professionals are watching two independent events unfold simultaneously.

FOREIGN INSTRUMENT TRADERS

Assume a foreign instrument trader buys a debt instrument of a foreign corporation. As with any debt instrument it pays interest periodically. That interest payment reflects a rate of return. The fair rate of return is determined by the marketplace's perception of the issuer and the current condition of that country's marketplace. When a U.S. trader buys the instrument, payment for it is due in the normal settlement cycle of that instrument's marketplace and payment must be made in that marketplace's currency. A trader purchasing a foreign instrument on a *trade date* must pay for it on the *settlement date.* Does the trader buy the foreign currency to pay for the purchase on trade date, the settlement date, or in between? An example will answer this question.

Example: A British corporation's debt, £1,000 (pound sterling) Sir Kevin Ltd 8% 2006, is trading at £1,000 pound sterling. If the bond was purchased in England, it would cost £1,000 and return £80 per year. On the trade date, the British pound sterling costs $1.80 U.S. per pound or $1,800 U.S. for the bond. By settlement date, the British pound sterling has fallen against the dollar so that the pound sterling only costs $1.75. The trader could have a $50 advantage if the currency was purchased at $1.75 instead of $1.80.

    If the foreign bond trader bought Sir Kevin Ltd at $180 ($1,800 per bond) and sold them domestically at $182 ($1,820 per bond), the true profit would be $70 per bond, not $20, as the cost to the trader is really $1,750, not $1,800. The proceeds of sale are $1,820.

Please realize, of course, that if the currency moved the other way, the trade could have resulted in a loss.

SUMMARY

    To recap, the value of a currency within a country fluctuates in value. This is commonly known as *inflation.* In a healthy economy this change goes unnoticed. However currencies fluctuate against each other more dramatically. It is this dramatic change which attracts industry participants to become currency traders.

    First there is the ability to trade the currency, itself. Then there is the ability to trade foreign securities which are to be paid for in either domestic or foreign funds. If they are to be paid for in foreign funds, the timing of when to acquire the foreign funds becomes important. Next there is the ability to trade derivative products on currencies. Some traders specialize in trading futures, others trade options, while still others trade both. Finally, there is the ability to trade all of the above. This combination of trading offers both the potential for profit and excitement for the international trader.

Chapter 11

Swap Traders

As stated throughout this book, traders exist because there is a need to exchange something for something else. An investor is buying securities in an attempt to increase wealth by exchanging cash or other securities. A farmer is selling a "future" on crops yet to grow and, in effect, is exchanging price risk and potential additional profit for the comfort of knowing a fixed delivery price. An investor exchanges bonds that pay interest every 6 months for a mortgage-backed security that pays principal and interest monthly, thereby increasing his cash flow. In assisting these participants in achieving their goals, the trader buys from one, sells to another positioning himself in the issues in an attempt to make a profit. In the trader's case, capital is being exchanged for inventory and risk is taken for the possibility of profit. Therefore, traders and their respective markets exist as long as there is a need to exchange issues.

This need to exchange issues or "trade" must be augmented by different interests. All interests in the same product cannot be on the same side of the market. Traders cannot exist in a one-sided market, as there isn't any place to lay off positions.

HOW SWAP TRADING WORKS

This book discusses many different forms of trading. Included in the products discussed are currencies and futures. Traders that conduct business in currencies are hedging one currency against another or one currency against a future or option. Those that conduct business in currency futures and/or options are positioning themselves based on expected or anticipated events that are yet to occur. In between these two, and an integral part of our lives, are interest rates. These rates affect intra- and intercurrencies users and, as such, develop a condition which requires the involvement of a trader. The trading of interest rates is generally known as *swaps*.

Swap traders perform an important function in the trading or "swapping" of interest payments. For example, a business has a 1-year variable rate loan. The lender is, therefore, receiving interest each month based on situations outside his control. The lender swaps the cash flow of the variable rate for one with a fixed rate. Depending on the movement of interest rates over time, the receiver of the fixed-interest payments may have an unexpected (though very welcomed) asset.

For example, one party of a swap has accepted a 3-year commitment to receive a rate of 11%. One year later, the going rate for this type of debt is 10%. The recipient of the 11% commitment can turn around a *sell commitment* for a premium or sell a 10% 2-year commitment locking in the 1% difference.

RISKS FACED BY SWAP TRADERS

There are many factors affecting the risks that swap traders face. First, if they have the two interested parties ready to trade the same or similar amounts at agreed-to terms, life is simple. However, more often than not this is not true, and the trader must carry one leg of the position for a period of time. This represents not only market risk to the trader, but also involves the expense of a cost of carry.

A swap trader must be very careful in matching swap commitments. Different instruments have unique or idiosyncratic features. For example, a 6-month T Bill discounted at a 10% rate is not the same as a certificate of deposit carrying a 10% rate. The T Bill discounted at a rate of 10% is, in effect, yielding a rate higher than 10% because the "discounted" interest is subtracted from the instrument's principal. The acquirer is paying less than "face" and, therefore, will earn more than the discounted rate. A certificate of deposit paying 10% is computed off its face and, therefore, pays 10%.

In matching floating-rate versus fixed-rate swaps, the behavior of the fixed-rate instrument has a dramatic effect on the risk/ reward potential. Parties to the contract must fully understand the terms, as "I thought you said," or "What I meant" cannot be tolerated. For example, if we do a swap "based on the 3-month T Bill," are we referring to the new 3-month bill with the rate being adjusted to reflect the next 3-month bill when this one expires; or are we referring to the weekly auction where the "fixed" rate is adjusted on a weekly basis as the new 3-month T Bills are auctioned in their usual cycle?

What if the contract expires on an off period? U.S. T Bills are auctioned on Monday, the results are announced on Tuesday, and the instrument begins to trade regular way on Thursday. If the swap commitment expires on Tuesday, which rate is used to determine Tuesday's cost? The previous T Bill rate or the new T Bill rate?

As with any tradable product, swap traders are exposed to market risk from product forces as well as from supply or demand caused by the market participants. For example, a swap trader's quote would be "30-year U.S. T Bond + 30 basis points to 30-year U.S. T Bond + 40 basis points." Assume the 30-year T Bond is yielding 9.50%, the quote becomes "9.50% + 30 basis points to 9.50% + 40 basis points." Suppose the trader has entered into a contract to receive interest at 9.50% + 40 basis points and while attempting to enter into a swap agreement with another party, interest rose so that the trader has to close the position or "hedge" the position and pay 9.60% + 40 basis points. The trader would have a loss.

PERCENTAGE AND BASIS POINTS: THE GROUNDWORK FOR ALL SWAPS

In order to fully understand the role of the swap trader, it is necessary to review percentages and basis points. One percentage point equals 100 basis points. Therefore, a rise (or fall) in interest rates a quarter of a point equates to 25 basis points. The term *basis* is short for the phrase *yield-to-maturity basis* as in "the bond is calculated on a yield-to-maturity basis." A swap trader giving a quote of "9.50 + 30 to 9.50 + 40" is really saying that he is willing to pay the yield to maturity of 9.80% (9.50% + 30 basis points) and receive a yield to maturity of 9.90% (9.50 + 40 basis points).

Like the traders in other issues, the swap trader is faced with two direct, but independent, forces affecting pricing. One is current interest rates, the other is the spread or amount of basis points (spread) the market will tolerate. The amount of basis points that can be added to the existing rate is dependent on current market conditions (competition and rate level); and in some cases, the creditworthiness of the trading party affects the basis points computation.

THE INTERCURRENCY INTEREST-RATE SWAP

The final form of swap which we should discuss is the *intercurrency interest-rate swap.* As discussed in the previous chapter, the relationship of currencies' values fluctuate against each other. Therefore, the rate of interest paid on loans within the respective currencies have different values as well. By swapping interest payment rates, the cost of borrowing could be reduced if the participant anticipated the movement of the currency correctly. For example:

1. One British pound (BP) equals $1.80 (U.S.).

2. The going lending rate in the United Kingdom is 11%; the rate in the U.S. is 10%.

3. Borrowing 100,000 British pounds would cost 11,000 British pounds interest. Borrowing the equivalent $180,000 U.S. would cost $18,000 in U.S. interest.

4. Therefore, 11,000 British pounds at the current exchange rate (£1.00 = $1.80 U.S.) equals $19,800 U.S.

It would appear, therefore, to be less expensive to borrow dollars in the United Kingdom than it would be to borrow British pounds. If you had dollars to lend, would you lend them in the United Kingdom at the equivalent rate of 9%? Probably not. You would lend dollars at a higher rate and increase your profit opportunity. For the sake of this discussion, let's continue with another example using the British pound and the U.S. dollar.

Suppose the loan was taken at the rates given above. At the end of loan, the dollar had risen against the British pound so that one British pound equaled $1.50 U.S.

1. The $18,000 U.S. equaled 10,000 British pounds when the loan was taken ($18,000 ÷ 180).

2. The $18,000 U.S. equaled 12,000 British pounds (18,000/ 150) when the loan was terminated.

As a participant in this market, had you swapped currency and interest pounds for dollars or just swapped the interest pounds for dollars, you would be facing a loss at closeout time. Let's review this one more time.

1. One British pound equals $1.80 U.S.

2. Instead of borrowing 100,000 British pounds, you convert (exchange) to dollars and borrow $180,000 U.S.

3. You now owe $180,000 U.S.

4. In order to close out the loan, you must repay the $180,000 which is the equivalent of 120,000 British pounds which

equals 20,000 British pounds more than you originally intended
to borrow.

This section concerns interest-rate swaps, therefore, had the
borrower of 100,000 British pounds swapped the interest-rate
payment for dollars, the swap would have cost 12,000 British
pounds instead of 11,000 British pounds, as required by the loan.

If, however, the loan's interest could be satisfied by the
payment of 11,000 British pounds sterling, the individual could
have swapped the British-denominated interest payment requirement for its dollar equivalent ($£11,000 \times \$1.80 = \$19,800$ U.S.)
and at the end of the loan period reversed the process by converting ($\$16,500$ U.S. $\times .66667 = £11,000$) $\$16,500$ U.S. to pay the
£11,000 owed on the loan. The remaining $3,300 U.S. would
be profit.

SUMMARY

The role of the swap trader has grown as globalization has
become more and more a reality. The service provided by these
swap traders plays a key role in international financing by giving
participants new dimensions of flexibility. As described above,
the tools are there and the decision process must be precisely
executed without any room for assumption. Each participant
must fully understand the terms being negotiated and what the
full ramifications of those decisions may be.

The swap trader, like any other trader, must be cognizant
of those events that affect the marketplace. Interest-rate swap
traders must keep on top of events that could affect floating rates
and then affect fixed rates; currency swaps must be concerned
about catastrophic events that could affect a nation, as well as
economic events both inter- and intranational. Finally, currency
interest-rate traders must make themselves aware of all of the
above mentioned events.

Chapter 12

Options Traders

Options traders generally use a very conservative approach to their trading strategies. Before we examine what and how these traders operate, we must first understand what options are and how their pricing works.

HOW OPTIONS AND OPTION PRICING WORKS

An *option* is a privilege to do something (buy/sell) if the *holder* (owner) so desires. If they don't want to do anything, they do not have to; it is the owner's "option." The *writer* (seller) of the option only has to perform the terms of the option contract if the owner exercises that privilege. The *buyer* pays the seller a premium for the option.

The terms of the option are explained in the contract specifications. *Equity options,* for example, are usually based on 100 shares of underlying stock whereas *index options* are for $100 multiplied by the index value. Each type of option product has its own quantity requirement.

All option products expire at some given point in time. Equity options expire the Saturday after the third Friday of the expiration month. The month of expiration is noted in the contract specification (i.e., the notation for January is Jan, April is Apr, August is Aug, and so on). The price at which the terms of the contract will be performed is also noted in the options description. For example, in equity options a strike or exercise price of 50 signifies $50 per share. As an equity contract is for 100 shares of stock, the value of the contract is $5,000 (100 shares × $50 = $5,000).

PUTS AND CALLS

As stated above, the terms of the options are explained in the contract. An option gives the owner the privilege to do something. That something may be the option to buy or the option to sell. When one owns the option to buy, the individual is said to own a *call* (the ability to call in the issue). When one has the privilege to sell, it is known as a *put* (the ability to put the security out). So, a call option gives its owner the privilege of buying if they want to, whereas a put gives the owner the privilege of selling.

Let's see how these options would work in with a few examples. A call on RAP Apr 50 means that the owner of the option can call in (buy) 100 shares of RAP common stock anytime the owner wants up until the Saturday after the third Friday in April. The price will be $50 per share or $5,000 for a round lot of stock (100 shares × $50 = $5,000). In order for this to be advantageous to the owner, the stock would have to be trading above $50.

A put on ZIP Oct 70 means that the owner can put out (sell) 100 shares of ZIP common stock anytime the owner wants until the Saturday after the third Friday in October. For exercising the put, the owner will receive $7,000, $70 per share on 100 shares sold. In order for the exercise to be advantageous for the owner, the stock must be under $70 per share.

These examples bring forth a key concept of options. Call options increase in value as the underlying issue increases in value, while puts increase in value as the underlying issue decreases in value. The relationship between the exercise price of the option and its underlying security value can be in one of three states at any one time. The option can be *out of money, at the money,* or *in the money.* If the current market value of the underlying issue is below the exercise price, a call is said to be out of the money. If the strike price of the option and the market value of its underlying issue is the same, a call option is said to be at the money. Where the strike price of the call option is below the market value, the option is said to be in the money.

In-the-Money Calls

One way to look at in the money calls is that the option has "intrinsic" value. For example, if you had been given a call with a strike price of 50 as a gift when the underlying security has a market value of 60, the call would be worth 10 points. The reason for this is that you could:

$$\text{Sell the underlying security } (100 \times 60) = \$6,000$$
$$\text{Exercise the call (Buy)}(100 \times 50) = \underline{5,000}$$
$$\text{10-point profit} = \$1,000$$

Therefore, at the point in time that the underlying security is worth $60, the call, with an exercise price of 50, would have an intrinsic value of 10 points (1 point = $1, so 10 points = $10).

In-the-Money Puts

Puts are the mirror image of calls and increase in value as the underlying issue value falls. If the underlying issue value is below the exercise price of the option, the option is in the money.

For example, if you were given a put at 50 as a gift when the underlying security was presently trading at 35, the put would have an intrinsic value of 15 points. You could:

$$\begin{array}{r}
\text{Buy 100 shares of stock at } 35 = \$3,500 \\
\text{Put out the stock at } 50 = \underline{5,000} \\
\text{15-point profit} = \$1,500
\end{array}$$

At-the-Money Options

An at-the-money call has a strike or exercise price equal to the underlying value. For example, if PIP is trading at 40, a PIP call with a strike price of 40, or in this case a PIP put would both be at the money.

$$\begin{array}{r}
\text{Call in 100 shares of PIP with a strike price of } \$40 = -\$4,000 \\
\text{Sell 100 shares PIP @ current market value of } \$40 = \underline{+\$4,000} \\
\text{Profit or loss} = 0
\end{array}$$

or

$$\begin{array}{r}
\text{Buy 100 shares of PIP with a current market value of } \$40 = -\$4,000 \\
\text{Put out 100 shares PIP with a strike price of } \$40 = \underline{+\$4,000} \\
\text{Profit or loss} = 0
\end{array}$$

Out-of-the-Money Options

Out-of-the-money options have no intrinsic value and, if exercised, would result in an immediate loss. These options trade on expected or perceived values known as time value. The more volatile an issue is, the better the opportunity that an out-of-the-money option could become an in-the-money one.

An example of an out-of-the-money call would be: if ZAP common stock is trading at 63, a call with a strike price of 70 would be out of the money as no one would exercise (call in) $7,000 worth of stock when it is only worth $6,300.

With ZAP at 63, a put with a strike price of 55 would be out of the money as no one would buy stock at 63 ($6,300) and put it out (sell) at 55 or $5,500.

Table 12.1. *Sample Option Quotes.*

Expire date Strike price	Sales	Open Int.	Week's High	Low	Price	Net Chg.	N.Y. Close
G M Feb40.....	1122	1071	$2\frac{1}{2}$	$1\frac{7}{16}$	$2\frac{1}{4}$	$-\ \frac{1}{4}$	$41\frac{3}{4}$
G M Feb40 p...	1386	1765	$1\frac{1}{4}$	$\frac{1}{2}$	$\frac{5}{8}$	$+\ \frac{1}{8}$	$41\frac{3}{4}$
G M Feb45.....	1153	2839	$\frac{3}{16}$	$\frac{1}{16}$	$\frac{1}{16}$	$-\ \frac{3}{16}$	$41\frac{3}{4}$
G M Feb 45 p ..	170	327	$4\frac{3}{4}$	$3\frac{3}{4}$	$4\frac{5}{8}$	$+1$	$41\frac{3}{4}$
G M Mar40....	1014	4857	$2\frac{3}{4}$	$1\frac{7}{8}$	2	-1	$41\frac{3}{4}$
G M Mar40 p ..	2494	6326	$1\frac{1}{2}$	$\frac{7}{8}$	$1\frac{1}{8}$	$+\ \frac{3}{16}$	$41\frac{3}{4}$
G M Mar45....	1378	18475	$\frac{7}{16}$	$\frac{1}{4}$	$\frac{5}{16}$	$-\ \frac{3}{16}$	$41\frac{3}{4}$
G M Mar45 p ..	648	3749	$4\frac{7}{8}$	$3\frac{7}{8}$	$4\frac{3}{4}$	$+1\frac{1}{8}$	$41\frac{3}{4}$
G M Mar50....	201	3462	$\frac{1}{16}$	$\frac{1}{16}$	$\frac{1}{16}$	....	$41\frac{3}{4}$
G M Mar50 p ..	398	949	$9\frac{7}{8}$	$8\frac{1}{4}$	$9\frac{1}{4}$	$+1$	$41\frac{3}{4}$
G M Jun40	739	1438	$3\frac{1}{2}$	$2\frac{7}{8}$	$3\frac{1}{4}$	$-\ \frac{3}{8}$	$41\frac{3}{4}$
G M Jun40 p...	615	1624	$2\frac{1}{2}$	$1\frac{3}{4}$	2	....	$41\frac{3}{4}$
G M Jun45.....	1038	2936	$1\frac{1}{8}$	$\frac{7}{8}$	$1\frac{1}{16}$	$-\ \frac{3}{16}$	$41\frac{3}{4}$
G M Jun45 p...	338	672	$5\frac{1}{2}$	$4\frac{1}{2}$	$5\frac{1}{8}$	$+1$	$41\frac{3}{4}$
G M Jun50.....	76	810	$\frac{3}{8}$	$\frac{1}{4}$	$\frac{1}{4}$	$-\ \frac{1}{8}$	$41\frac{3}{4}$
G M Sep45 p...	166	211	$6\frac{1}{8}$	$5\frac{5}{8}$	$5\frac{7}{8}$	....	$41\frac{3}{4}$

p = Put
Calls are unidentified

Look at Table 12.1; which options are in the money? Which are out? Remember, if you obtained the option free and exercised it for a profit it is in the money. If an exercise resulted in a loss, it is out of the money.

Factors Affecting Puts and Calls

Intrinsic Value and Time Value and Their Effects on Puts and Calls. Included in the price of an option, therefore, is its *intrinsic value*. To sell an option for less than its intrinsic value would mean an immediate profit to the buyer. Premiums of options usually trade at full intrinsic value and more.

The premium of an option is made up of intrinsic value and time value. Intrinsic value is synonymous with the in-the-money sum. *Time value* is primarily comprised of the issue's volatility. In other words, what the underlying issue can achieve in this marketplace during the life of the option. The more "time" remaining in the option, the more opportunity the underlying issue has to change value.

The Affect of Market Volatility. In addition to intrinsic and time value, other factors affect the price of the underlying issue. *Market volatility,* in general, describes the perception of the industry in which the underlying issue is a part, the economy in general, the amount of the strike price, and, of course, current interest rates. Another term for interest rates is cost of carry. Interest rates determine what it costs (what the expense is) to carry a position from day to day; or if the position didn't exist, what would be the return of the money invested in a riskless investment. The higher the interest rates, the higher the time value.

The Affect of Premiums. To better appreciate the affect of premiums on calls and puts, a basic understanding of how they are treated is in order. Call premiums must be added to the options strike price to determine the break-even point, while put premiums must be subtracted from the options strike price to determine its break-even point.

Example: A purchaser of a call with a strike price of $30 and a premium of $3 would have a break-even point of $33. This means that if the underlying issue was trading at $33 in the last moments of the options life, the option would be worth, intrinsically, 3 points. The underlying issue would have to be at a higher value in order for the option to be profitable.

If, in the above example, the option was a put, then the underlying issue would have to be at $27 in the last moments of

Figure 12.1. Purchase of a call @ $3 with a strike price of $30.

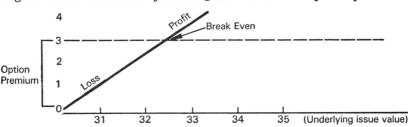

Figure 12.2. Purchase of a put @ $3 with a strike price of $30.

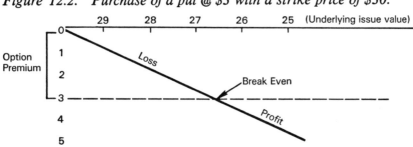

trading in order for the put owner to break even. If the underlying issue was trading below 27, the option would be profitable.

As demonstrated in Figures 12.1 and 12.2, the amount of time value commanded by the marketplace is critical in the trader's decision process because of its direct implications on the break-even point.

THE OPTIONS' PREMIUM VALUE

One of the most difficult concepts to grasp in trading options is the relationship of the movement of the *options premium value* to a one-point move in the underlying issue. As premiums contain time value and time value represents volatility or potential underlying movement, opinions premiums change as time erodes the time value. In addition, if prices were checked on a vendor's screen or in the newspaper, one would see that out-of-the-money options move less in relationship to a one-point move in the underlying issue, whereas in-the-money premiums move considerably more.

Example: POP common stock is trading at $30 per share. POP has an April call options trading on it with strike prices of 25, 30, and 35. Let's assume that the marketplace agreed that POP common stock could reach $34 by expiration. The premium for the three options would be 9, 4, and 0 ($25 + $9 = $34, $30 + $4 = $34, and the $35 strike price option would be worthless).

A worthless option! What if the stock rises above 34 and reaches 35½; what if the consensus of the marketplace is wrong? On the other hand, the 25 and 30 strike price options are both priced to the same point. If you believed the stock could go over $34, which option would you buy? If the options underlying issue closed out at expiration at $35, the 25 strike price option would be worth 10 and the 30 option would be worth 5, so:

The $25 strike price option is now 9 points; at maturity it will be 10 points for an 11.11% return.

The $30 strike price option is now 4 points; at maturity it will be 5 points for a 25% return.

Another factor to consider is that if POP, in fact, fell from its current price of $30 to the price of $25 by expiration, the buyer of the $30 call would lose 4 points, whereas the buyer of the $25 call would lose 9 points. In addition, the interest cost in carrying a $900 option is more than double that of the cost of carrying the 4-point option.

Based on the above, the $30 strike price call option is more attractive than the $25 strike price option; the prices would reflect it. If, in fact, the 30 strike price option was trading at $4, the $25 strike option would be trading below $9. For the sake of this example, we could assume a price of about $7.

Let's look back to our "worthless" option. By it having no value, the entire marketplace would have to think that there is no way the stock could break through $35. If one person thought that it could, many people (who think it can't) will be willing to sell that person the option, maybe at a price of ¹⁄₁₆ or at ⅛. This would probably be pure speculation; but if the stock moved through $35 to $35½ at expiration, that option would expire with a value of ½. If it is worth $12.50 now, it will be worth $50 at expiration which, in turn, equals 400% in return. (Trade with your head, not your heart!) The reason for the high return is the high risk that was taken. In all probability, this option will go out worthless. If the risk wasn't this high, others would also be buying the option and the price would be higher.

Let's assume that some time has passed and the stock rises from 30 to 31. The aforementioned options are older and have less time left to their life. Which option would reflect this 1-point move more to the greatest extent, the 25, the 30, or the 35? In all likelihood, the 25 would which was trading at 7. With the underlying at 30 and a premium of 7 (5 points intrinsic value, 2 points time value), the option now has 6 points intrinsic and a 1-point time value. The 30 option now has 1-point intrinsic value and a 3-point time value, and the 35 option is still at an "all time" value of 1/16 or 1/8.

Assuming the marketplace's perception remains at $34 per share by expiration, the 1-point move in the underlying issue would have its greatest effect on the most expensive option; the one with the greatest percentage of intrinsic value and the least amount of time value. The effect that a 1-point move of the underlying issue has on an option premium is called its *delta*.

Deltas range from 0 to 1 with 0 having no effect and 1 being $1 for $1. The deltas of each option series differ. The deltas between options products differ, as well. Deltas are a function of volatility, either real or perceived.

Understanding Option Premiums

To reiterate, options are tools, and tools in the hands of fools are accidents. As the terms of the options contract are standard, the point of concentration is therefore the premium.

Understanding premiums is understanding the tools of a good trader. Understanding the tools is to know which one to use in a particular situation. Before you can understand the tools, you must understand some basic aspects of the workings of those tools within the scope of the marketplace. These facts are:

1. Calls increase in value as the value of the underlying issue increases. They fall in value as the underlying issue decreases. Puts work in reverse.

2. In an "it's going to go up" stock situation, you would buy calls or sell puts. In an "it's going down" stock situation, you would buy puts or sell calls.

3. If you own an option, the most you can lose is the acquisition cost of the option. If you sell or write an option, the maximum profit is the premium received at the time of sale.

4. If the market perceives that a particular stock has the ability to fluctuate, the amount of perceived movement would be reflected in the time portion of the premiums of the option.

5. As options are a contract, the stated value at which services will be performed is found in the option's strike price. The difference between the strike price of the option, the market value of the underlying issue, and the time value of the premium develops the profit or loss potential. One of the three components are fixed (i.e., the strike price) and the other two are dynamic.

The word *dynamic* is used because changes are not reflected in the premium on a $1 for $1 basis. Traders are sensitive to these relationships and relate them to rates of return.

Let's integrate the five points. As the underlying issue rises in price, the intrinsic value of the overlying call rises, but the intrinsic value of the put falls.

Example: RIP increases in value from $30 to $40. The intrinsic value of a call option with a strike price of $30 has gone from $0 to $10. The intrinsic value of a put option with a strike price of $40 has gone from $10 to $0.

If the underlying issue falls in value, the intrinsic value of the puts increase and the calls decrease. How about the other side of the coin. Instead, let's assume the stock value fell from $40 to $30. A put with a strike price of $40 would have its intrinsic value rise from $0 to $10; whereas a call with a strike price of $30 would have its intrinsic value fall from $10 to $0.

In establishing good strategies, it may be helpful to study the following maximums, regardless of how unlikely the events:

Buy a Call

Maximum profit	The underlying infinite market value minus strike price, minus premium
Maximum loss	Acquisition cost of option

Buy a Put

Maximum profit	Strike price minus premium, minus underlying market value (when value is 0)
Maximum loss	Acquisition cost of option

Write (sell) a Call

Maximum profit	Sale proceeds from options
Maximum loss	The underlying infinite market value minus strike price, minus premium

Write (sell) a Put

Maximum profit	Sale proceeds from options
Maximum loss	Strike price minus premium, minus underlying market value

To demonstrate the above list of basics in mathematical terms, let's assume two individuals, Stephan and Mack, are entering into an option trade. The first option is a call on Varga Cosmetics, Inc. expiring in July with a strike price of $45. The option is trading at $7, Varga Common stock is trading at $48. In its current mode, the marketplace is saying that, in this option series, Varga could reach a market value of $52 (strike price $45 + premium $7 = $52). If the option was exercised at this point, the owner (buyer) would be losing 4 points. The cost of the option is 7 points which will pay on the call exercise $45 which is equal to $52. (Market value of stock equals $48; $52 − $48 = 4 points.)

If Stephan buys the call, he is predicting that the stock is going above $52. If Mack were to sell the call (go short, or write) he would be saying that the stock will not reach $52.

Table 12.2 shows what the possibilities are for Mack and Stephan. Say Stephan bought the option from Mack for 7 points (7 times 100 shares = $700). If the option expires worthless, Stephan will lose a maximum of 7 points and Mack will earn 7 points. The option will expire worthless if the market value of the stock, in this case Varga Cosmetics, is at or below $45 at expiration.

If, however, Varga Cosmetics rises in value from $52 to $70, Stephan will earn 18 points profit ($80 − [Strike Price $45 + Premium 7] = 18 points). Mack would lose 18 points. If Varga rose above $80, Stephan would earn even more and Mack would lose more.

Finally, if Varga common stock "goes out" between $45 and $52, Stephan would reduce his loss, but Mack would earn less. Let's assume that the stock "goes out" at today's value of $48; Stephan who paid 7 points would lose 4 points as the option

Table 12.2. Possible Call Options for Varga Cosmetics, Inc.

Stephan's	Mack's	Market Value
Profit = 18 pts.	Loss = 18 pts.	$70
(Strike price $45, option worth $25 ($70 – $45 = $25)		
Profit = 8 pts.	Loss = 8 pts.	$60
(Strike price $45, option worth $15 ($60 – $45 = $15)		
Profit or Loss = 0 pts.	Profit or Loss = 0 pts.	$52
(Strike price $45 plus premium of $7)		
Loss = 7 pts.	Profit = 7 pts.	$45
(Strike price $45)		
Loss = 7 pts.	Profit = 7 pts.	$40
(Option worthless)		

would still be worth 3 points (market value $48 – strike price $45 = 3 points), Mack would earn a 4-point profit only as Stephan would exercise or Mack would simply buy one option back in at a price of 3.

Let's look at puts. Stephan is about to acquire puts on Varga Cosmetics, Inc. with an expiration in July and a strike price of $45. Let's assume Varga common stock is trading at $42, and the option is trading at 6 points. (See Table 12.3.)

If Stephan exercises the put, 100 shares of Varga Cosmetics would be delivered by Stephan and he would receive $4,500. As the option cost $600, Stephan's *net* is $3,900. As Mack

Table 12.3. Possible Put Options for Varga Cosmetics, Inc.

		Market Value
		$60
Stephan's Loss = 6 pts.	Mack's Profit = 6 pts.	$50
Stephan's even	Mack's even	$39
Stephan's Profit = 9 pts.	Mack's Loss = 9 pts.	$30
Stephan's Profit = 39 pts.	Mack's Loss = 39 pts.	$ 0

acquired the stock for $4,500 and received $600 for selling the put, his net is $3,900. Ergo, 39 is the break-even point.

Included in the premium is not only the volatility of what the underlying issue is capable of, but also what problems the market, in general, can cause. Quiet markets, over time, will be reflected very little in the value of premium; whereas volatile markets would show some influence on the premium. The same is true in market direction. Upward movement would tend to inflate call prices, while downward movements would tend to inflate the price of puts. Because of these market directions, it is possible to "pick" the correct strategy, but lose money because of the influence of the market on the premium.

The more sensitive a stock is to the market movements, the greater the volatility that will be reflected in the premium. The method of measuring a stock's movement in relation to the market (its volatility versus the market's over time) is known as the stock's *beta*. A beta is defined as a measurement that quantifies the correlation between the movement of a stock and the movement of the stock market as a whole. A stock with a beta of more than one will have a higher volatility; a stock with a beta below one will have less. Betas are also one of the tools option traders have in determining what their perception of an option premium should be.

Using the beta or volatility is a double hit. First, as the market's volatility increases or contracts, it has an influence on the option premiums. Second, as the stock reacts to the volatility, it has an effect on the premium. For example, the market has been very calm; it then becomes volatile. As each stock is either causing or reacting to this change, the option premiums will reflect the increased risk. On top of this, the amount the stock is moving in relation to the market is further reflected in the premium. Here's an example of what could happen to a stock in a volatile market:

Example: Rainbow Ltd. has been trading in a 34 to 36 range for two months. The market (Dow Jones Industrial Average) has been in a 30-point range for the same period. Suddenly, the Dow drops 30 points, then 50 points, then 60 points in three consecutive trading days. What if Rainbow's stock value falls 1 point, 1 1/2 points, and 1 ¾ points over the same period? What affect would the above scenario have on the put or call premiums of Rainbow's options? What if Rainbow's stock fell ⅛ point, ⅜ point, and ½ point? Would that have any effect on pricing the option? What if Rainbow actually increased in value during the 3-day period? What effect would this have on the premium?

Volatility is the issue's market value ability to change over brief periods of time. Beta is the ability of one issue to track another issue over time.

Example: Two stocks are trading at $10 per share in January and at $40 per share in December. One stock had a steady upward trend. The other fluctuated drastically over the same period of time. The second stock would have a higher volatility than the first. (See Figure 12.3.)

Figure 12.3.

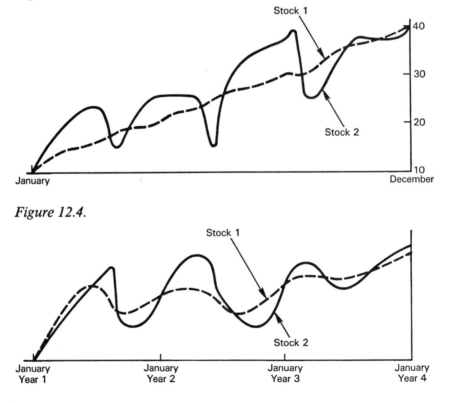

Figure 12.4.

Beta is the ability of one issue to track a second issue over time, the degree to which one issue moves along with another. If the second stock out moves the first issue the beta is above "1." If the second stock doesn't out move the first issue, the beta will be less than "1." (See Figure 12.4.) Stock 2 would have a beta above "1" as it follows stock 1 but out moves it most of the time.

THE TRADER'S ROLE IN THE OPTIONS MARKET

Now that you have a clearer understanding of premiums and their effects on options (especially the time value of the premium), you can get a better understanding of how option traders think and work.

For example, traders perceive that any recent activity in a security is over-rated and that the recent volatility will calm down. The trader would sell options and wait for the volatility, or time value, of the option to shrink. For example, weeks after the October 1987 market move, option premiums in certain products were reflecting exaggerated time values. As confidence was restored, the time value condensed. Traders who sold these options made profits even if the underlying issue's price remained the same.

In the same vane, because the premiums were so inflated, individuals anticipating certain events occurring that would affect the value of the underlying issues would take option positions when the event occurred and the underlying issue would react. When the event occurred, the price change did occur, but the premium actually contracted because the shrinking of anticipated time value was greater than the effect the event had on the option premium.

OPTION STRATEGIES

Now that the basics of options have been presented, it is appropriate to examine the different strategies which are employed.

Buying Calls

The expectation is that the underlying issue value will increase during the term of the option. The break-even point is the strike price of the call plus the acquisition cost of the option. The maximum loss is the acquisition cost of the option. (For simplicity, all costs and expenses are omitted.)

Example: ZOW is trading at $38. A $40 strike price call is trading at $3. The break-even point is $43 (equal to the strike price plus the premium). The profit at expiration would be figured as follows: If ZOW is trading above $43 (i.e., ZOW is trading at $50, the option would be worth 10 points ($50 market value minus $40 strike price = 10 points) minus 3 points cost equals 7 points profit). The maximum loss would be equal to the acquisition cost of the option (in this example, 3 points). If the stock closes at $40 or below, the option expires worthless. Loss is, therefore, the cost of the option.

Buying Puts

The expectation is that the value of the underlying issue will fall. Break-even is the strike price of the option. The maximum loss is the acquisition cost of the option.

Example: PAW is trading at $48 per share. A $50 strike price put option is trading at $5 (the premium is comprised of 2 points intrinsic value and 3 points time value). If PAW is trading below $45 at or before the option's expiration, you would have a profit. Let's assume PAW is trading at $41 per share at expiration; the option would be worth 9 points (theoretically, the option owner could buy the stock at $41 and put it out (sell) the stock at $50 per share with the option's strike price for a 9-point profit). With the option worth 9 and an original cost of 5, the option owner would earn 4 points.

If break-even is $45 per share, the stock would have to be selling at $45 at the options maturity for the owner to be assured of breaking even. At that point the option would have an intrinsic value of 5 points (the acquisition cost).

If the stock is trading above $50 per share when the put option expires, then the option is worthless and the owner loses the original investment.

Selling (Writing) Calls

We are now on the opposite side of the previous two explanations and are, therefore, also on the opposite side of the market expectation. Selling calls anticipates a downward market. Selling puts anticipates an upward movement. When selling or "writing" options, the maximum profit is the proceeds of the sale. "No one" at "no time" at "no place" is going to give the writer any more money than at the time of trade.

As stated above, selling calls anticipates a downward movement in the market because the "writer" wants the option to expire worthless, thereby leaving the "proceeds of sales" intact. For call options, break-even at expiration is determined by adding the strike price of the option and the premium together. Once the stock value exceeds the original premium plus the strike price, the writer of the call option is in a loss position because the cost of buying the option to close out the position would be greater than the proceeds of the original sale.

In options, as in futures, it is as easy to sell a contract as it is to buy. To open a contractual position which is a selling transaction (aka, *short* or *writer*) is commonplace. It is usual to have both writing (selling) options where you have the underlying in position (known as *covered*) and where you don't (known as *uncovered*). The previous paragraphs concerned the writing of *uncovered calls;* the next paragraphs are concerned with *uncovered puts.*

Selling (Writing) Puts

The writer of uncovered puts is anticipating an upward movement in the underlying security. As with calls, the proceeds of sale are the only revenue the writer will receive. It is, therefore, the writer's objective to purchase the put at a later date at a lower price, or better yet, have the option expire worthless.

The break-even point for a put writer is when the underlying issue reaches the value of the strike price minus the acquisition cost of the option (i.e., a put with a strike price of $50 is sold for 3 points). If the underlying falls to a price of $47, the writer is even. If someone puts the stock to the writer, the writer will have to pay $50 per share as specified in the contract, and then would likely turn around and sell the stock in the market place at $47 per share (the stock's current value).

If the value of the underlying issue fell below the break-even point, the writer would be facing a loss. If the stock were to fall to $42 per share by expiration, for example, the put option would be worth 8 points. Since the writer received 3 points when the option was sold, the writer would be facing a 5-point loss at expiration (8 points value at maturity minus 3 points premium received when sold equals 5 point loss).

It must be noted that the form that most of the listed products use is the *American form of option.* This means the option can be exercised anytime during its life. The other form of option, known as the *European form,* can only be exercised at the end of their life. As the majority of option products traded are in the American form, a writer with an in-the-money option may be exercised against or assigned at any time the position exists.

Holders of domestically listed options exercise their contractual privilege against the *Option Clearing Corporation* (OCC), the issuer and guarantor of listed options. The OCC then takes the exercise and assigns it, on a random basis, to a writer or written position. Therefore, writers must be cognizant of the fact that they may be assigned at any time, thereby closing out the position.

COVERED WRITING

Most traders never enter into large single positions. They are cognizant that while they want to make a killing in the market, the market has the ability to "kill" them. Therefore, traders use various forms of hedging to protect themselves against loss. One of the most basic forms of hedging uses covered writing. This allows the trader to own the stock and *write a call* against it.

The premium received from the option serves to increase the rate of return or to lower the break-even price of the long stock position.

Example: RAZ is trading at $48. A 3-month RAZ option with a strike price of 50 is trading at $2. Buying 100 shares and selling one call results in:

> The break-even price for the stock being $46 (48 minus 2 points for the option).
>
> The maximum profit being 4 points because the stock will probably be called away at $50 per share if stock rises above that $50 price. ($50 per share minus $48 cost per share equals 2 points, plus 2 points received from the option equals 4 points profit.
>
> The return if the option expires worthless would be $200/4,600 = 4.34%. The return if the option is exercised would be $400/4,600 = 8.69%

Traders pay very close attention to the option series' delta. As stated earlier, delta is the amount the option premium will move as compared with each move point of the underlying issue. Traders also know the option deltas will change as the option moves in or out of money. The deeper an option moves into the money, the higher its delta will become. Also, the closer an option gets to expiration, the greater will be the volatility of the option premium. For example, in the last moments of trading before an option expires, the delta is either zero (if the option is out of the money) or one (dollar for dollar) if the option is in the money.

If the $50 strike price call, mentioned above, was about to expire and the underlying stock moved from $48 to $48 1/8, the effect on the out-of-money option would be nil, or a delta of zero. The option is worthless. If, however, the stock was trading at $52 and moved to $52 1/8 in the last minutes of the option trading, the premium would move from $2 to $2 1/8 (dollar for dollar) for a delta of one.

Traders also know that the volatility of the underlying issue or changes in the movement of the underlying issue over short periods of time can also occur, which in turn changes the option series delta.

Traders, therefore, attempt to magnify rates of return by the use of a strategy known as *ratio writing.* If the delta was "25" on the $50 strike call, the trader may buy 100 shares of stock and sell 4 calls with the $50 strike price. The trader is anticipating little or no movement in the underlying issue. As the option gets older, the premium will decrease allowing the traders to buy back the options at lower prices and writing new ones for additional return.

In addition, as the underlying stock rises *over time,* the amount of time value is dissipating. Therefore, when the stock eventually reaches $50, the premium of the $50 call, because of erosion in its time value, may be 1 point. With the stock at $50, the delta may be "50" or higher, which means the option price will increase ½ point for every point the underlying rises. At this point, the trader may close out the position. Let's look at a ratio write broken down into steps.

Buy 100 shares of stock at $48 = $4,800
Sell 100 shares of stock at $50 = $5,000
$ 200 profit

Sell 4 call options at $50 strike price at 2 points = $ 800
Buy 4 call options at $50 strike price at 1 point = $ 400
$ 400 profit

Your gross profit before expenses = $600

The optimum profit could be obtained if the option expires worthless with the stock closing on the last day of that series trading at a price of $50. Here's the calculations for that profit:

Sell 4 call options with a $50 strike price @ 2 points   = $ 800
Expiration of 4 call options with a $50 strike price @ 0 =   0
$ 800 profit

Stock bought at $48 = $4,800
Stock sold at $50   = $5,000

+ $ 200
$1,000 profit

However, should the stock have a sudden move upward, the trader would have the four options working against him. Remember the delta was .25 which means that at that level, a 1-point move of the stock would cause a 25 cent ($\frac{1}{2}$ of a point) move in the option, multiply this by 4 and you have a $1 move in the option. Any event which can throw the equilibrium off, especially an increase in the delta or volatility of the option, could throw the trader into a loss position.

Covered Writing Puts

Selling stock short and then selling puts is another covered writing strategy. For example, the trader will sell short 100 shares of stock at $52 and sell the appropriate number of puts against the position. Again the trader is anticipating little movement in the underlying issue. A small downward movement would be preferred so that the options will expire worthless and the trader will have a small profit from buying the stock back. Assume the option delta for the $50 strike price put is 40. The trader would

Sell short 200 shares at $52;

Sell 5 puts (500 shares $\times$ .40 = 200 shares); and

Assume a premium of $1\frac{1}{2}$ = $750

If the stock falls to $50 at the expiration of the option, the option will be worthless ($750 profit) plus $200 profit buying the stock in at $50 (sold short originally at $52).

If the stock rises, the puts will lose value. The stock can rise $3\frac{3}{4}$ points (multiply by 2 to equal $700 on 200 shares) before the short sale becomes a loss. If the stock is trading between $52–$55$\frac{3}{4}$, the trader will not incur a loss. If the stock closes at expiration between $52 and $50, the traders will retain the $750 premium plus any difference between the short sale of $52 and the "buy-in" price ($50–$52).

If the stock closes below $50, the trader would be facing losses as for each point being earned on the stock would be offset by losses on the puts. As a matter of fact, as the stocks drop below $50, the options "go into-the-money" and the trader could wind up being long (owning) 300 shares (200 short shares + 500 put shares for a net long of 300 shares).

SPREADS

By definition, spreads involve the simultaneous purchase and sale of equal numbers of puts *or* calls having the same underlying issue and different series. In spread strategies, one position is the primary position, the other is either a risk or cost reducer.

$$\left.\begin{array}{l}\text{B 1 call ROW Oct } 40 = 5 \\[4pt] \text{S 1 call ROW Oct } 45\ = 2\end{array}\right] \text{ 3 debit}$$

Spreads are traded at *net debits* or *credits*. In the above spread, the long call is trading at 5, the short call is trading at 2, for a debit of 3. Spreads are traded at a net price. It is the difference between the cost of the option being purchased and the procedures received from the option being sold.

In this spread, the long option is the main option, the short option serves as a reducer of the "long's" premium. Let's assume that the underlying issue was trading at $40 and was expected by the trader to rise to $45 by the time the option expired. With the $40 strike price and option trading at a premium of $5, should the trader be accurate in his perception, then the premium paid for the option (5 points) will be what the option is worth at expiration. Therefore, the other "leg" of the spread reduces the "cost" of the long option to 3 points. If the trader is accurate, then the stock will be selling above $45 by expiration, resulting in a profit of 2 points. The long option will be worth 5 points; the short option will be worthless.

It must be noted at this time that if and when the stock rises above $45, the profit made on the long option will be offset by losses on the short option. If, for example, the stock was to rise to $48 by expiration, the $40 call would be worth 8 points; the short $45 call would be worth 3 for a net of 5 points. As the position originally cost 3 points, the liquidation of the position during any time at a 5-point spread would still result in a 2-point profit.

Another type of spread is when the secondary option is used as an "insurance policy." For example:

Sell 1 put ZAP Oct 50 = 4 ⎤
                          ⎥ 3-point credit
Buy 1 put ZAP Oct 45 = 1 ⎦

The written option is the main option in this position. The trader believes the ZAP will rise in value and/or stay above $50, thereby rendering both options worthless. But what if the trader is wrong and the stock falls in value? The short put will gain in value. To minimize the "cost" of a wrong decision, the trader has purchased a $45 strike price put which minimizes the loss to 2 points.

In the above example, the trader is anticipating that the underlying issue (ZAP, in this case) will rise and that the ZAP Oct 50 Puts will expire worthless, so that he can keep the premium. If, however, the ZAP stock was to fall in value, the trader would have exposure and face a greater loss than the justified premium. To maintain some level of acceptable exposure, the trader bought the ZAP Oct 45 Put which reduces his loss possibility to 2 points. This type of "trade off" is very prevalent in option trading. How important is it for the trader to earn 4 points when 3 points, with the assurance that the maximum loss will be only 2 points is possible? Is the possibility of earning 1 point worth the possibility of losing everything?

The terms *horizontal, calendar,* and *time spreads* refer to the similar types of spread strategies where the expiration months of the options vary. An example would be:

Buy 1 put ZOW Oct 50

Sell 1 put ZOW Jul 50

Vertical, price, and *money spreads* refer to types of spread strategies where the strike prices are different.

Buy 1 call WOW Jun 45

Sell 1 call WOW Jun 50

Diagonal spreads have both different expiration months and strike prices. And, last but not least, *ratio spreads* are designed to operate in the same fashion as ratio writing. Ratio writing was discussed in the previous section.

STRADDLES AND COMBINATIONS

A *straddle* is defined as the simultaneous purchase or sale of equal numbers of puts or calls having the same underlying security and the same series description. For example:

Buy 1 call ZIM Oct 50 = 3

Buy 1 put ZIM Oct 50 = 2

What this strategy is telling us is that the owner doesn't care which way ZIM common stock is moving; the owner of the straddle just wants ZIM to move up or down more than his 5-point cost by the time the option expires. He could also be looking for ZIM to move, pricewise, with greater volatility so that the premiums will increase within the time value so that the position can be closed at a profit.

The seller (or writer) of a straddle is expecting very little movement in the underlying security. While the possibility of retaining *all* of the premium is remote, the trader is expecting to retain some of the premium. In order to retain all of the premium, both the options would have to expire worthless and the stock could not move too far away from the strike prices because of the exercises against the writer.

Combos or combinations are similar to straddles but, at least one of the options in combination, either the put or the call, must be out of the money. This reduces the cost to the buyer and reduces the risk of being exercised on both options during the life of the position. Option traders use these strategies as well as variations on them in conducting their business.

These professionals come under special rules. The individuals or the firms they are employed by must be registered with the Securities and Exchange Commission as broker/dealers. If they trade on a floor of an exchange, they must take qualifying examinations as well as arrange for membership on the exchange. If they trade from an "upstairs" trading desk, they must be deemed qualified by passing the National Association of Securities Dealers (NASD) examination and/or an exchange examination. As you can imagine, these trading positions come under different requirements than do retail nonbroker dealer margin requirements. They, therefore, have greater latitude and financial flexibility in the conducting of their trading.

As with other products, there are two main goals of a trader or market maker. One is to earn a living, the other is to stay in business. Therefore, most traders hedge their positions and then monitor them from minute to minute. In the following examples, for brevity's sake, we do not know or care what strategy the opposing side of the trades are utilizing; we only know what a trader may do. In addition, we are looking at trading on a micro level and not a macro level, which is the way traders operate in reality.

Traders are generally armed with the following information:

How the stock relates to a given stock index.

How sensitive it is to interest-rate changes.

How volatile the stock has been over a given period.

How the stock relates to the common stock of companies in the same related industries.

How much activity there is in the underlying stock (i.e., volume of shares traded daily).

How much activity there is in the options themselves.

What the prognosis is for the economy *or anything* else that could affect the price of the underlying stock.

Each of the above statements are important to the trader and have a direct bearing on how a trader manages his activity. For example, if the option is very active, a trader may buy a given series and then turn around immediately and try to sell it at ⅛ or ¼ of a point higher (attempting to earn $12.50 or $25.00 per option). However, someone else may have just offered an option for sale at that price which causes the trader to do one of two things. First, he could offer it as well and wait for the priority offer (first offer) to be filled. Second, he could reoffer it at the price paid, thereby getting out of the option position "even" (minus processing costs). If the trader believes it is a "good buy," he may enter into a position in another series, thereby creating a spread, straddle, or combination which changes his focus from trading in and out quickly to trading premium differences. (Bear in mind that it is as easy to sell an option for a profit as it is to take a loss.) Traders will always seek to minimize losses. A trader can go out of business proving that he is right in his strategies. This is a lesson the public should practice. These are business transactions, not a test of your integrity or brilliance.

Sometimes traders take positions using the options to *box* the movement of the stock. For example:

B 1,000 MAP at 80

S 10 calls MAP Apr 80 = 3

B 10 puts MAP Apr 80 = 2

In this ideal situation, the sale of the calls will "bring in" $100 per option or $1,000 over the cost of the puts. If the stock pays a dividend while the position is "on," the trader will be paid that as well. During the period the position is maintained, if the price of the stock rises, it will be called away. If the stock falls in value, the trader can "put" it out. Either way, the stock will leave the position at the same price at which it was purchased. This strategy is known as *conversion*.

The reverse of this position is also an effective strategy. Take for example:

Sell short 1,000 MAP at 80

B 10 calls MAP Apr = 3

S 10 puts MAP Apr = 2

In this strategy, the trader is borrowing stock and using cash as collateral against the loan. The entity receiving the money (collateral) is willing to pay the trader interest on that money. The trader faces no exposure on the stock position and if the stock rises, the trader will call it in; if the stock falls in value, someone will "put" to the trader, either at the price of the short sales. The trader is responsible for any dividends paid during the period the short sale is in force.

THE BRIDGE INFORMATION SYSTEMS

"Volatility, volatility, when I'm sure I understand you, I discover that I really don't." Thanks to Bridge Information Systems, Inc. we are able to review the market price movement of the common stocks of five well-known companies for the past 6 months. They are in alphabetical order. We have selected these five out of the many available on the Bridge network.

American Telephone and Telegraph

General Motors Corporation

International Business Machines Corp.

NYNEX

UAL Corporation (United Airlines)

Study the charts in Figure 12.5 through Figure 12.9. Look at the different time periods being reflected. Look at the NYNEX chart (Figure 12.5) and take it from May to July and from August to October (two 3-month periods). In the first period, the stock's value fluctuated about 12 points. In the second period, the range is one-half that amount. It is as if you were looking at two different stocks. Someone buying options during the first period and expecting the movements to continue, probably overpaid for the option. The time value portion of the premium for the first 3 months would carry the continued volatility expectation. But as the second 3 months passed, the time value of the given option would decrease.

UAL Corporation is involved in a buyout. (See Figure 12.6.) In the past 6 months, the stock has fluctuated from 110 to 300 and down to 160. By the time you read this, the result of the

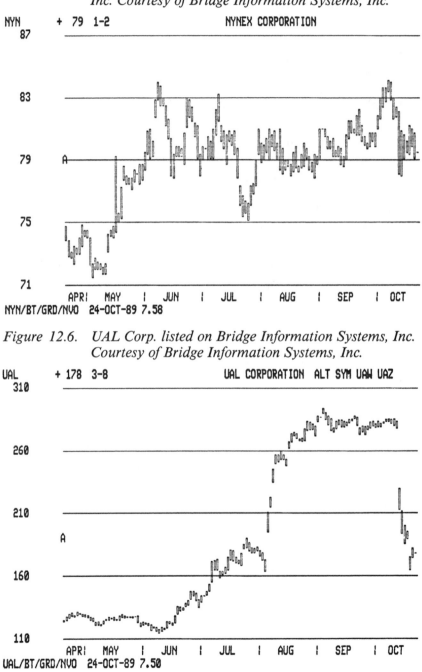

*Figure 12.5.   NYNEX Corp. listed on Bridge Information Systems,
Inc. Courtesy of Bridge Information Systems, Inc.*

*Figure 12.6.   UAL Corp. listed on Bridge Information Systems, Inc.
Courtesy of Bridge Information Systems, Inc.*

buyout attempt(s) will be known. Who was right, who was wrong; only time will tell. However, at this writing if you were setting "fair value" for UAL Corp., how much time value would you want for a 3-month option (call or put)?

Now let's focus on the General Motors chart in Figure 12.7. Over the 6-month period, the stock has ranged 10 points and is basically selling for the same price in October as it was in April. The periods of time are important as the stock's movement has been sporadic, ranging from daily fractional changes to swings of a few points at a clip. From the chart presentation in Figure 12.7, you could assume that the stock was leveling off and trading will be in the $45 to $47 range for a while. You can check the actual price movement of GM by consulting your newspaper for the 52-week high and low.

The chart for American Telephone and Telegraph in Figure 12.8 presents a "textbook" picture of security movement. The spread over 6 months is 12 points on a base of 33 with very few aberrations of any size from day to day. That changes, however, in

Figure 12.7. General Motors Corp. listed on Bridge Information Systems, Inc. Courtesy of Bridge Information Systems, Inc.

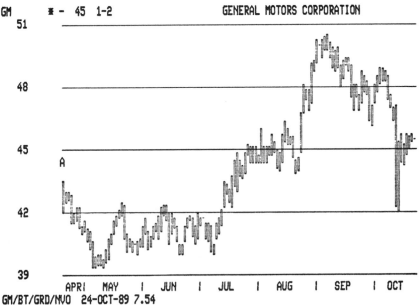

October as the stock registered some comparatively wild swings, thereby upsetting the volatility computation. As the volatility changes, so does the delta which, in turn, affects the premium.

Delta, as mentioned earlier, is the amount the option series premium changes in relation to a change in the underlying issue. For example, an option with a delta of 25 means that its premium is expected to change by ¼ of a point for each point the underlying's market value changes. A delta of 12 will have the effect of ⅛ premium change to each $1 move of the underlying. Generally, as the option series relationship to the underlying move from out of the money to deep in the money, the delta will rise and vice versa.

Finally, study the IBM chart in Figure 12.9. For almost 6 months the stock traded within a 16-point range. Over a shorter period of time, the range was less with some months averaging 3 points or less. Then suddenly in September, the stock began a downward plunge. From mid-August 1989, when the stock was

Figure 12.9.   IBM listed on Bridge Information Systems. Courtesy of Bridge Information Systems, Inc.

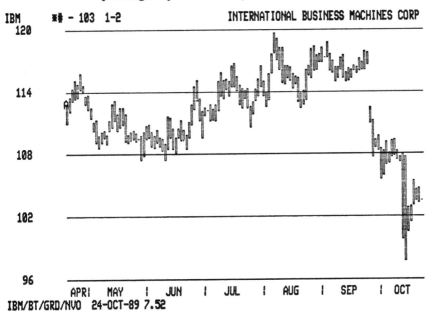

trading at close to 120, to mid-October (2 months), when the stock traded at approximately 97, is a 23-point move.

The five stocks each have their own story, their own history and, therefore, their own projected future. It may be helpful in understanding time value if you check the current market value of these issues.

SUMMARY

As stated previously, traders must master several strategies and know when to employ them. Based on market conditions, a trader may use one options strategy or several at one time. These strategies may have to change from moment to moment. Each strategy requires individuals who are executing orders against individuals who, in turn, are instituting or closing their own strategies affecting other individuals, and so on and so forth.

Chapter 13

Futures Traders

The world of futures is a fascinating world of contracts that establish prices at which a delivery of an item will occur at a later date (at some date in the future) ergo, its name *future*. Because it is used to establish some future delivery, the buyer and seller of the contract will not become involved with the contracted product until it becomes deliverable. Therefore, the money involved per contract is small, usually around 5 to 10% of the contracted amount, in relationship to the full contract value. This relationship of good faith monies (5 to 10%) versus the contract size gives the trader a lot of leverage per dollar. This leverage could produce either large profits or large losses very quickly. Practitioners in the futures market must master the relationship between risk and reward early on in their careers in order to survive in the marketplace.

HOW FUTURES TRADE

To understand the futures trader, one must understand the futures product. A future is a contract specifying the delivery of a specified quantity of the underlying issue at an agreed to price and on a specific date. Whoever has sold the contract must *deliver* the issue, under the terms of the contract. Whoever bought the contract must receive the issues under said terms. To put it simply, a future sets the price today at which a delivery will take place in the "future."

As the future contract represents a commitment to be fulfilled at a later date, the amount of capital necessary to carry the position is small in view of the total contract size. This capital generally runs about 5% or less for a traders unhedged position. The full contracted value is not required until the delivery is made. In between the time the contract position is established and it is closed out, either through trading or delivery, the position(s) are *marked to market* (a written notice stating the issue's current position) after the close of business each day. Therefore, the profit and/or loss potential in trading these instruments looms larger than most other products.

Unlike equities or debt instruments, these products can be sold before they are purchased as easily as they can be bought originally. It is as usual to have sold (short) positions as it is to have bought (long) positions. Remember, the seller owes the buyer the product and the buyer owes the seller the price. Because this practice of selling contracts before ownership is such a normal way of conducting business, the term used to close out, or trade out, a position is liquidate. The expression used is, "the position was liquidated." Owners of long positions liquidate by selling while owners of short positions liquidate by buying.

To better illustrate this concept, let's concentrate on two people, Farmer Green and Miller Gray. Farmer Green is about to plant seed. The farmer is concerned with the costs in growing the crop and the price to be received at harvest. Costs of growing cannot be guaranteed because of all of the variables involved (weather conditions, equipment leasing, and so on). Cash received for the crop can be guaranteed because there are futures trading on that very crop which will serve to protect one side of the equation. Farmer Green would sell future contracts on the crop, thereby locking in the price.

Miller Gray also has concerns. Primarily, these include the cost of the inventory (crop), the processing costs, and the selling price. Futures allow Miller Gray to lock in the cost of his inventory by purchasing contracts.

If both of these individuals maintain their respective positions until delivery, they will be conducting business at the agreed-to or contracted price. By locking in the contract price, both Farmer Green and Miller Gray have given up the possibility of profiting more from advantageous price movements, but they have also given up the possibility of loss through market price activity.

Let's use the wheat crop contract as an example. The wheat contract is comprised of 5,000 bushels. Wheat is selling at $3 per bushel. Let's suppose the total costs to the farmer to grow and harvest the crop was $2.25 per bushel. If the market price of wheat falls below the $2.25 per bushel price at the time the wheat came to market, the farmer would have invested all this work for a loss. However, let's assume that with wheat at $3 a bushel, a miller can earn 3 cents a loaf of bread. If the price of wheat rose per bushel, the miller would have to raise his price per loaf. This price rise could reduce the demand which may leave the miller with excess wheat resulting in a loss.

The farmer and miller are in business to make a profit and, therefore, must hedge their risk when possible. As the originator and the end user of the wheat cycle, they establish future positions when they perceive it to be advantageous in order to lock in the delivery price. The individual that they will probably be trading against is the future trader.

Since the farmer and miller lay off or transfer market exposure or risk to the trader, what kind of person is this risk taker? Is he suicidal? Does he drive a nitroglycerin truck? Skydive without parachutes? Why would someone be willing to take on someone else's risk? Futures traders accept this risk because they are also trying to layoff or transfer risk in their trading strategies.

HOW FUTURES EXCHANGES WORK

Before we discuss the types of futures traders, it is important to understand the futures exchanges, the trading methodology used, and the key participants in the futures market. *Futures exchanges* use an "open outcry" method of trading. While the highest bid and lowest offer has the floor, no one has priority. This is unlike equity exchanges where the first bid at the highest price and the first offer at the lowest price have priority. As a holder of this priority, these orders must participate in the first execution at those prices. As priority doesn't exist on the futures floor, the traders and brokers continuously call out the highest bids or lowest offer. As there is no priority, no one is monitoring who made the highest bid or lowest offer first; the participants with the highest bid or lowest offer just continue to call out their markets and, therefore, the trading process is named "open outcry."

The traders and brokers in the "crowd" are very cognizant of the prices being called out. A trader bidding or offering is also listening to what others are calling out. If, for example, Pat Dino is bidding "55" and the quote is "55 to 65," Dino must change her quote or be silent should someone else bid "60." The question Dino must ask herself is, do I want to own this at "60" or should I sell this at "60" to the bidder and try to buy it back at "55," my original bid?

In this market environment, futures trade in *pits* or stepped-circular rings. The market makers stand in the pits or on the lowest platform with brokers standing on the steps that surround the pit. This arrangement exists because the brokers must maintain visual contact with their phone clerks located around the outside of the pit who are hand-signaling orders and other instructions received via the telephone from member firms or member firm clients. The broker accepts orders and gives back reports through the use of these hand signals. Later, paper or electronic versions of these orders are developed and then are actually entered into process.

Market makers trade for their own account and, therefore, have no need to be in constant communication with a phone clerk. By standing inside the pit, the trader has a panoramic view of what is happening. They know who is bidding, who is offering, and the current size (amount) of the contracts that are available at those prices. In addition, floor traders know the crowd. They know the brokers and have a pretty good idea of the customers that the brokers are representing at a given moment in time.

THE DIFFERENT TYPES OF FUTURES TRADERS

Scalpers

The first type of trader to be reviewed is known as a *scalper.* They are nonpositioning market makers. They go in and go out of positions as quickly as possible. For example, the quote on a given future that trades in "nickels" (5-cent intervals) is $21.20–$21.25; the trader buys the contract at $21.25 and immediately offers it at $21.30. If no one takes it, he/she will reoffer at $21.25. If there is no taker at $21.25 they will offer it at $21.20 and take the loss.

The art of being a scalper is predicated on being 100% mental at all times and *never, never* letting emotions enter the decision process. Scalpers earn their revenue by simply making profits on more transactions than those they take losses on. By "emotions," I mean an ego problem that says "I'm right, I know I'm right, they are wrong; I'll show them." Even if the market price of the future being transacted eventually turns and heads in the direction the trader wants, it's not worth the exposure. To jeopardize one's capital, to put it simply, is just not worth the risk. For a scalper, there is no need to prove greatness if he wants to be in business tomorrow. If a position is taken and the market goes the other way, the scalper gets out.

Scalpers, basically, use market trends or directions to trade. By buying and selling, selling and buying, they add a degree of depth to the market by accepting risk from moment to moment. Scalpers, in conjunction with other traders, form a base for the trading of larger orders by taking on smaller portions of the order and then from time to time reoffering or acquiring these pieces in the marketplace. For example, 10 market makers trading 5 contracts each against an order for 50 contracts is as good as a 50-contract trader.

Hedgers

In addition to the scalpers, there are *hedgers*. Hedgers will "lay off" the risk of one position by trading against another position which they are maintaining. They may go long one delivery month contract while shorting another if the price difference between the months look attractive. Hedgers also "lay off" risk against similar or related products. A soybean trader, for example, knows the relationship between the future products traded (i.e., soybean, soybean oil, and soybean mash). As the market price relationship between these future products gets out of line, the hedger will take offsetting positions and wait until the abnormality corrects itself.

In addition, options contracts are traded on some of the underlying future contracts. These put and call products are available on many future products and add a new dimension in trading as traders will "lay off" one position against the other and, again, against the other. The option would be used in the same manner as it is in equity options with the deliverable on exercise being the future.

Hedgers generally concentrate on products with which they are familiar. Because of the hectic pace and potential price movements, the traders stay near the pits (downstairs) or near the phone (upstairs) while they have positions on the floor. In visual contact with them at all times are the various news and vendor services that keep the trader advised on what is happening in the particular product. The various news items that appear in rapid succession may or may not have an effect on the trader's position. The hedger tries to determine what effect, if any, the news article will have on the product and makes adjustments, that is, trades to increase or decrease the position.

Market Watchers

At times a trader will take market action in the reverse of an expected result of a news article. This will occur when the market appears to be overbought or oversold in relation to the effects of a news story. A dramatization of this is the term *panic selling*. In other words, the market participants have overreacted to a condition that has affected the market in a negative way. The value falls way below the product's fair value. Some traders will buy during this situation.

"No pain, no gain" is an expression used by not only futures traders but position traders of all products. To be a successful trader, the individual must take chances, must take risks. It is the understanding of the risk and the potential reward which are of paramount importance. With this understanding, traders will "take chances" and take on contrary "to the current opinion type positions" when they believe that if they are wrong, the exposure is minimal, or at least acceptable. This type of trading strategy is not for the novice or ill at heart. To be successful at it, you must be correct on two counts. One is your opinion of market movement; the second is your opinion of what the market will do if you are wrong.

For example, Troy Bahrs is a gold trader who has a long position in gold futures at the present time. Troy knows that OPEC is going to meet within the next 2 months to try and set the price of oil at $18 per barrel. Oil is trading at $16.50 per barrel. If OPEC is successful, the $18 a barrel price could set off inflation worries, which in turn could cause the price of gold to rise. If OPEC is not successful, oil prices may remain at their current levels or fall, causing gold prices to perhaps weaken.

The trader, while increasing and decreasing the contracted position through trading, is maintaining an overall long posture and, assuming all other influences remain status quo, will structure the size of his long posture on what can be lost if the OPEC meeting does not reach agreement.

If Troy believes that $16.50 a barrel is fair price and will be unaffected should OPEC not succeed at setting the $18 a barrel price, he may be willing to assume a much larger overall position than if he believes that $16.50 a barrel has been influenced by the pending OPEC talks. In other words, should the talks not occur, or if the OPEC meeting ends in disarray, the price of oil may drop. The accurate reading of the possible negative outcome is as important as the anticipation of the positive. This is a major consideration and contributor to the success and/or longevity of a trader. "But what if I'm wrong?" must be a question truly addressed and answered honestly. No one likes to think about failure. We all prefer to think in degrees of success. A trader, especially a futures trader, (where profits or losses can be determined by events outside the control and/or understanding of human beings (i.e., weather)) must address "what if I'm wrong?" as often as "what if I'm right?" In other words, being wrong comes with the occupation. It happens. When it does occur, the trader should cover the loss (get out of the position) as soon as possible and go on with the business at hand.

In the summer of 1988, there was a growing concern as to the possibility of a drought affecting the Midwest. Soybean prices, as well as other agricultural products, climbed almost daily. In 1 month, the nearby month soybean futures contract rose from $7.65 a bushel to $9.10 a bushel. That's a rise of $1.45 per bushel. As the soybean future contract is designed for 5,000 bushels, an individual who opened a position with 1 contract in 1 month and closed it out in the following month dealt with a profit (if bought first and then sold) or a loss (if sold first and then bought) of $7,250. A 10 contract position would be a profit or loss of $72,500.

Some of the above price moves happened gradually; at other times it was caused by a "run." Because of the ability of contract prices to move with such force, suddenly and sometimes without warning, and due to the relatively low margin required, a unique process unfolds in the futures market. This unique feature, which is found in certain futures products, is that they trade within a *value range*. If the price exceeds the range (either up or down) on a given day, trading is halted. This halt is deemed necessary to permit traders and clients of commodity firms, who deposit very little equity (market) per futures contract at the time of trade, to deposit additional funds. As the futures market value moves up or down, the positioners either profit or lose. When the position is losing money, the positioner will be called for additional equity which must be deposited immediately. To give the representatives firms an opportunity to rebalance the positions and to collect the money, trading is halted.

The process may occur over 2 or 3 consecutive days, during which time it is possible that a positioner is locked in to an issue he may not want to remain in.

Example: Let's develop a product that has a price movement limit of 30 cents the first day, 50 cents the second day, and 80 cents the third day. The product trades in 2 cent intervals and the contract contains 10,000 pounds of our product which is currently trading at $3.46 per pound. The margin required is 10% or $3,460 per contract. As a trader, you purchase 10 contracts at $3.46 with the expectation of closing the position out in the $3.50 range or at whatever the price is one-half hour later, whichever occurs first. If it reaches $3.50 within one-half hour, you will earn a $4,000 profit.

Suddenly some bad news breaks and the market tumbles more than 30 cents before you can liquidate your position. The next day it falls 50 cents, and, on day three, the price falls the full 30 cents. It opens on the fourth day "down" $1.60 (30¢ + 50¢ + 80¢) at $1.86 per bushel. The $1.60 per bushel drop has cost you $160,000 ($1.60 × 10,000 bushels × 10 contracts). Naturally, the same series of events could have happened in reverse and you could be up, or profiting $160,000.

How could the trader have protected against a disaster like this? First, the trader would know what products or futures trade in a relationship to this future (i.e., a severe drop in this product's market value was caused by a news event). That event may have affected other future products. The trader could have tried to offset the exposure by using the other product. Some future products will cause a negative or reverse effect on what are apparently unrelated products. An example would be if the price of lumber drops which causes home construction to become less expensive which, in turn, causes the price of homes to fall which, in turn, increases the demand for homes, which increases the demand for money, which increases interest rates, which makes overall borrowing more expensive, which means bond prices fall as yields rise, and so on leading to investments in gold causing the price to rise and so forth.

Some product's prices will cause perspective substitute product's prices to become competitive. Using a previous example, if the price of lumber rose instead of fell, at some point the cost of wood could reach a price level that would make steel, plastic, or any other substitute material desirable. Even wheat, if it rose in price to where the public could not afford or did not think the price of a loaf of bread was reasonable would see a slacking off of demand as substitutes, such as corn meal and/or potatoes, pick up the slack and filled the need for starch in our diets. To be a successful position trader in futures, one must know what the alternatives are.

Index Futures Traders

Index futures were introduced in the early 1980s as a method of hedging stock portfolios. Soon after, options on index futures were introduced along with options on the indexes themselves. This product caught the community's interest and, in turn, offers the knowledgeable trader a vast array of products to trade.

First, there is the future itself which can be traded against another delivery month of the same index. Then, there is the possibility of trading one index future against another (i.e., S&P 100 against the NYSE Composite). Traders can also trade the future against the option on the future, the future against the option on the index, or the future against a basket of stock which has been developed to replicate the index itself, and so on. The combinations and permutations are astounding. Confused? Let's run through this again.

An index future sets the price today against which the index will be settled at some time in the future. As the stock index fluctuates, so does the perceived value of the future. At present, physical securities cannot be delivered for settlement of these future contracts and, therefore, settlement is affected in cash. What is owed is the difference between what the contract settlement calls for and the closing value of the index at the contract's maturity. For example, an individual owns a future contract and the closing value of the index on the last day of trading is higher than the contract value. The owner of the future receives the cash difference. The seller would have to pay the cash difference. If the index value is lower, the buyer would pay the seller the difference. Unlike other futures, no product is delivered.

Index Futures Options Traders. Options on futures are very similar to other option products. There are puts and calls with fixed contract terms. When the trader exercises this type of option he becomes involved with the future contract. The exercise of a call will result in the option owner becoming the owner of the particular futures contract whereas the exercise of a put results in the option owner delivering or owing the future. The exception to this is when the option is exercised at its expiration, which occurs at the same time as the future enters its delivery cycle. As the future becomes deliverable and the option expires at the same time, exercise of the option at expiration involves the receipt and delivery of the future's underlying or, in the case of index options, cash.

Options on the index, itself, is a cash settlement on exercise. Except for that difference, index options follow pretty much the same structure and trading methodologies of other options mentioned elsewhere in this text.

Cash Settlement Products versus Physical Settlement Products. This is important! There is a major difference in the trading mechanics of cash settlement derivative products (futures and options) as there is for physical settlement derivative products. The difference is that the physical can and often does change value, whereas in the case of the cash settlement, it doesn't.

Example: A U.S. T Bond future becomes deliverable and the owner of the future receives and then pays for the U.S. T Bond. The next day, fluctuations in interest rates cause the T Bond to change value. In the case of a cash settlement, once the future becomes deliverable, the buyer and seller settle the cash difference and that's the end of it. Whatever the index does, valuewise, after settlement is not important as no one owns the index.

To focus on this difference another way, let's extend the above example. Now let's say that the T Bonds are owned. The individual can sell the next deliverable future against the bond position and be completely hedged (protected from loss with no possibility of profit) and collect interest on the bond (futures do not pay interest). You cannot hedge in this manner with cash settlement index futures. Therefore, what do index futures traders do?

A trader in index futures, as a trader in any other product, has many sources of information available and many conduits to trade through. It is important to note that an index future can be above (at a premium) or below (at a discount) the current index value. Whatever that perceived value is, it will merge with the true index value at the end of the particular futures existence.

Example: Let's assume WOW index is at $350.65. A future contract with 3 months remaining before delivery is trading at $352.50. As the dollar value of the future contract equates to $500 times the index value, the sum being discussed is $176,250 or a premium of $925 over the actual index value. If the index does not change value, or if the index should be at the $350.65 value when the future terminates, a short position established at $352.50 would receive $925 from the clearing corporation. Let's assume, however, that the index rose to $355.80 by the time the 3-month future ceased to exist. The short at $352.50 would pay the long at that price of $1,650 ($355.80 × 500 = $177,900, $352.50 × 500 = $176,250, $177,900 − $176,250 = $1,650).

A futures trader, in the above example, goes into the marketplace and trades a one lot. Even though it represents approximately $175,000, it is considered a small trade for most markets. Most traders, of course, deal in larger size transactions. Remember, these are future contracts setting the price today for delivery in the future. The trader must only deposit a small percentage of the contracts value to carry the position.

While we are on the subject of contract size, let's take a look at the size of some other future contracts.

Gold = 100 troy ounces @ $450 per oz. = $45,000

Soybean = 5,000 bushels @ $7.25 per bu. = $36,250

Coffee = 37,500 pounds @ $1.50 per lb. = $56,250

British Pound = 62,500 pounds @ $1.70 per £ = $106,250

Swiss Franc = 125,000 francs @ $.60 per F = $75,000

U.S. Treasury Bill = 1,000,000 dollars @ 92¢ per 100% = $920,000

U.S. Treasury Bond = 100,000 dollars @ 90¢ per 100% = $90,000

As it becomes evident, the dollar value underlying each future contract varies deeply. In addition, the ability of the particular product to change value (volatility) varies greatly also. Put these two facts together and then translate the result into profit or loss dollars, and an entirely new picture emerges. For example, a $100,000 valued contract that usually changes within a range of 3% has the same exposure dollar wise as a $50,000 valued contract that usually changes within a range of 6%. In other words, you can lose or earn as many dollars in the less volatile future as you can in the more volatile one if the size of the contract offsets the difference in volatility.

Of course, the reverse is true; a larger valued future contract with a higher volatility will out "move" a smaller sized contract with less volatility. A trader naturally must be cognizant of the difference.

Index Futures Trading Strategies. Getting back to index futures, the trader can be considered a scalper or a hedger, as is the case in most of future products. As a hedger, the trader can use other months of the same product, another index product, options on the future, or options on the index hedge.

For example, let's say that the marketplace is bullish. This sentiment will be reflected in the various index products. The products, trading in their own environments, will relate to the stimulus differently. Traders will buy and sell the different products, setting up different strategies based on the idiosyncrasies of each marketplace. For example, a trader could go long 10 future contracts and short 50 in-the-money index option contracts on the actual index. As stated earlier, an index future contract is usually five times the size of the option contract. The option on the future, however, is the same size as the future contract itself. Therefore, the trader could:

Be long 10 future contracts and hedge the position by selling (going short) call options on the future; or

Buy 10 put options on the future against the long future contract position.

The index future trader may decide to offset the 10 contract position against a position in another "month" contract. The strategy of "playing" one month against another usually involves pricing discrepancies. For example, based on the price of the nearer month future and a carrying charge of X%, the next expiring months future should be trading at Y. It isn't. Therefore, to a trader the problem must be that the near-month contract price is incorrect, the far-month contract is incorrect, or the "rate" is wrong. In any event, a trader will buy the one that appears undervalued, sell the one that appears overvalued, and wait for the correction to take place. If it does, a profit will result. If it doesn't, the trader may be "even" or have a loss.

Some future traders will compose a portfolio of stocks (known as a *basket*) that will replicate a particular index and use it to hedge an index futures position. For this concept to work, the trader must maintain large security and future positions. The trader waits for the index future to rise or fall to a converted interest rate greater than the cost of carrying the position. The trader buys the portfolio and sells the future or vice versa. For example, the WOW index is at $350.65 and the 3-month future has gone to a discount equivalent of a rate of approximately 9%. In other words, at this moment in time, the marketplace is pessimistic about the outlook for the economy. The future is trading *below* the current index value. The trader can *borrow* stock to effect short sales at a cost of carry of 6%. The trader can borrow the stock in the proportion necessary to replicate the index movements and sell it short. At the same time, future contracts can be purchased to offset the short sale.

As the index and the portfolio of stock will track each other dollar for dollar, the trader is not concerned with which way the market value may move. At the end of the future's existence, the index future contract and the index itself will have the same value. As the portfolio or basket has followed the WOW index dollar for dollar, its value change equals changes in the WOW index. The trader is, therefore, left with the 3% difference between the 9% discount and the 6% cost of carry.

To present this numerically, let's assume the WOW index is at $350.65 and the 3-month future is trading at $342.75. As the future contract calls for a value $500 times the index, each contract covers $171,375. The index itself, $350.65, must be multiplied by $500 to determine the amount of underlying value needed ($175,325). The trader buys 100 contracts at $342.75 (or

$17,137,500 worth of value) and sells short stock with the equivalent dollar value of the index at $350.65 (or $17,532,500). For the 3-month period of time the stock (valued at $17,137,500) will cost 6% or $257,062.50. At the end of the 3 months, the index future and the index have lost their differential and are now equal. The difference had a value of $395,000; the trader has a profit of ($395,000 – 257,062.50) $137,937.50. Of course, before you jump at it, this is simplistic and meant for exemplar purposes only. Missing from the equation is the expenses involved with the future, dividends owed on the borrowed stock and, perhaps the most important, the risk that the basket of stock stops tracking the index. This last point can be the biggest detriment to this type of trading.

Currency Future Traders

Currency traders operate from the close confines of the futures trading pits to a broad world of financial type instruments. While this may sound obvious, it is still important to understand the fact that currencies are legal tender somewhere on Earth. It would be difficult to buy something using wheat, gold, or index products as a method of payment. However, currencies, such as the British pound, the legal tender in the United Kingdom, and the Italian lira, the legal tender in Italy, fluctuate against the dollar as well as fluctuating against each other. Take, for example, the dramatic fall the dollar has had against the yen. To offset the volatility of the dollar against European currency, international currencies were developed. They are known as European currency units or ECUs. Traders can trade their component parts against this unit, as well.

Example: A British pound sterling contract is comprised of 25,000 pounds. With the pound worth $1.90, the contract is worth $47,500. At the writing of this book, the range for the pound over the life of the maturing futures was $1.90 to $1.53 which means the dollar equivalent is $47,500 to $38,250 for a difference of $9,250.

The Japanese yen is comprised of 12.5 million yen per contract and its range is .008390 to .006735 for a dollar equivalent of $104,875 to $84,187.50 for a difference of $20,687.50.

The German mark contract has 125,000 marks per contract and the range of the maturing contract is .6494 to .5410 or a dollar equivalent of $81,175 to $67,625 for a difference of $13,550.

Let's assume that all the currency highs and lows against the dollar occurred at the same time. If one purchased the pound contract at its low, the return is 24.1%. The yen would have returned 24.5%, the mark would have returned 20%. In the above example, the foreign currency in two out of three cases rose 24+% against the dollar with one rising only 20%. If this event is considered normal, then we have some interesting trading tools. A trader could hedge the yen by offsetting positions in the pound sterling. However, in using the German mark, one would need to compensate for the differences through the utilization of additional contracts.

All other things being equal, traders who purchased futures in these three contracts, sold them, and then repurchased them, would have made a nice profit. Traders who believed in the trends (chartists) and read the data correctly, stand a better chance, as they could buy on weakness and sell on strength. In other words, acquire contracts when they "looked cheap" and sell when they "looked overpriced."

Question: Who was better off by the aforementioned currency move, an individual who contracted to buy and pay in dollars, or the seller to the contract who will receive dollars? To answer this question, let's take the dollar versus the pound, for example. When the contract was formed, one British pound sterling was worth $1.53. Therefore, something made in the United Kingdom and sold in the United States which had a value of £10,000 would cost $15,300 stateside. If that was what the contract called for, a payment of $15,300 per unit would be expected on delivery. But what would happen if the pound was suddenly worth $1.90? The buyer may have made out better than the seller because the seller would be delivering units for $15,300 which should have a current market value of $19,000 (£10,000 × $1.90).

In the above scenarios, both the buyer and the seller could have protected themselves against financial adversity by "taking on" offsetting future positions. Had the seller of the 10,000

British pound sterling product bought a futures at $1.53, then the loss of 37 cents per pound would have been offset by the profit on the future contract. The buyer could have hedged the risk exposure (as though it was a profit) by selling the future.

It must be remembered that to hedge means to protect oneself against loss usually by the willingness to sacrifice profit. If in the above example the contract in dollars was determined by the rate of exchange at the time of delivery ($1.90), the seller would be whole, but the buyer would be acquiring merchandise that may be too expensive to sell.

SUMMARY

As you now know from reading this chapter, the life of a futures trader can be exciting and profitable if the proper strategies are utilized. The marketplace offers many vehicles for the futures trader—options, indexes, currencies, and so on. If the futures trader can keep his emotions in check and use the strategies discussed in this chapter, he may indeed profit in this fast-paced and everchanging market.

Conclusion

Still interested in being a trader? Any product of particular interest to you? Remember, the subject matter carried in each chapter represents a smattering of the material available. It represents an introduction to the topic only. Many books have been written on each topic and in many cases, books have been written on topics within topics. For example, there are books on bond trading, then to the level of corporate bond trading, then on to the level of introduction to yields, then on to yield analysis, then on to effect of different stimuli on yields, and so on. Books written on the topics cover, either directly or indirectly, the gamut of related subject matter.

We have reviewed the environment from equities through debt instruments, through currencies, into options, and finally discussing futures. It is an exciting world, regardless of the issues selected. Some are "hot" while others are "cold" and vice versa. It changes from day to day, hour by hour, minute by minute.

Unfortunately, we only hear about the ridiculous, absurd, or unusual situations. To the many who perform these functions and whose names never appear in the press, it is a way of life, a method of earning a livelihood. They match their skills and talents in a marketplace, buying and selling, selling and buying, making a marketplace for the you and me of this world to put in and out of positions.

To those readers who do not want to be traders but were curious as to what traders do, we hope the book has been beneficial. The aim of the book was to clear away some of the falsehoods or myths that exist about this segment of the industry.

If the text has explained the world of the trader and the difference between these specialists, then it was a meaningful effort. If it whetted your appetite and you pursue more in-depth understanding, then, and only then, has this effort been a success.

Glossary

A & O. April and October. Refers to the semi-annual months that a particular debt instrument pays interest. *See also* J & J, F & A, M & S, M & N, and J & D.

Accrued Interest. The amount of interest owed since the last payment period. It is usually paid by the buyer to the seller at the settlement of a transaction.

Acid Test. An accounting measure used to test the financial strength of a company. Acid test is accomplished by dividing current assets and quickly converting them into cash by current liabilities.

Adjustable Rate Mortgages. *See* ARM.

ADR. *American Depository Receipt*. A receipt issued for foreign securities on deposit at American banks. ADRs are domestically traded.

Agency. (a) Transaction executed on a broker basis. The broker acts as a conduit between the buyer and seller.

(b) Term used for federal agencies such as the GNMA, FHMA, FHLMC, the Bank of the Cooperatives, etc.

All or None. An instruction on an order that mandates that the order be completed in its entirety during the time allowed or the originator does not have to accept any part of it.

American Depository Receipt. *See* ADR.

American Form of Option. An option which can be exercised at any time during its life.

American Stock Exchange (AMEX). Regulated by the SEC, this exchange offers facilities for the trading of equities, options, and debt securities. It is one of two primary option exchanges.

AMEX. *See* American Stock Exchange.

Annualized Yield. What the rate of return would be if it existed for a one-year period of time.

AON. *See* All or None.

ARM. Adjustable Rate Mortgages. This mortgage's rate is "pegged" (tied) to some other rate and changes as the pegged rate changes, as permitted under the terms of the mortgage.

Ask Price. *See* Offer Price.

At the Money. Term used in options trading to signify that the underlying issue's value is the same as the option's strike or exercise price.

Away From Me. Execution occurring with other dealers.

Away From the Market. An order to buy or sell having a limit price not near the current market value.

Bankers Acceptances. A short-term debt instrument used in international finance.

Basis Point. $1/100$ of a percentage point.

Basis Price. Synonymous with yield to maturity. Used in certain instruments as a reflection of price.

Basis Spread. The difference in the yield to maturity between two debt products.

B/D. *See* Broker/Dealer.

Beta. The volatility over time of one product against a product with similar characteristics.

Bid Price. The part of a quote which represents the highest price any buyer is willing to pay for the standard trading unit.

Book Value. An accounting method for assessing a value to shares of stock based on the information contained in the company's balance sheet. It is *not* the same as market or par value.

Boston Stock Exchange. Registered with the SEC. Offers facilities for trading equities.

British Pound Sterling. Currency of Great Britain.

Broker/Dealer. A registration requirement with the Securities and Exchange Commission to conduct business in SEC regulated issues.

Broker's Broker. A firm whose clients are other firms and assists them in the buying and/or selling of issues.

BSE. *See* Boston Stock Exchange.

Buy/Write. Option strategy employing the purchase of stock and the selling of calls on the same security.

Callable. Situation where the issuer has the ability to retire (call in) the issue under the terms of the call provision.

Call Option. Gives its owner the privilege of buying the underlying security at a predetermined price for a specific period of time.

Canadian Dollar. Currency of Canada.

Cash Dividend. A distribution of cash paid by the company from earnings or retained earnings, on a per share basis, to its stockholders.

Cash Market. Term used in futures when the future contract is in its last month and going for delivery.

Cash Settlement. Settlement of transaction is satisfied by cash instead of a physical instrument.

Cash Settler. When the trade date and settlement date are the same day.

CBOE. *See* Chicago Board Option Exchange.

CFTC. *See* Commodity Futures Trading Commission.

Cheap. *See* Undervalued.

Cheapest to Deliver. Term used in certain products which permit several different issues to be delivered in settlement of a transaction. Due to pricing sensitivity, one instrument that qualifies for delivery will be the cheapest to deliver.

Chicago Board of Trade. Registered with the CFTC; offers trading facilities for commodity future trading such as cotton, soybeans, and so on; also future products such as T Bonds and T Notes.

Chicago Board Option Exchange. One of two primary option exchanges regulated by the SEC.

Clearing House Funds. Next day money; checks deposited on day one are good funds on day two.

Closed-end Mortgage Bond. Subsequent issues on the same property are junior (have a lesser claim) to the closed-end issue.

CME. Chicago Mercantile Exchange. Regulated by CFTC; offers facility for trading livestock (cattle, hogs) and products such as lumber.

CMO. Collateralized Mortgage Obligations. A securitized group of mortgages that pay principal based on tiers or tranches.

Collateralized Mortgage Obligations. See CMO.

Collateral Trust Bond. A corporate bond secured by securities of another issuer.

Combination (Combo). Simultaneous purchase or sale of equal numbers of puts and calls having the same underlying, but different, series designation.

Combo. See Combination.

COMEX. New York Commodity Exchange. Trades futures on certain precious metals.

Commercial Paper. Short-term debt of a corporation usually issued with maturities of one year or less.

Commodities Futures Trading Commission. Federal agency regulating the futures market.

Common Stock. Shares of ownership of a corporation usually containing the right to vote for the Board of Directors and on key issues facing the corporation management.

Conversion. A feature contained in certain issues that permits the issue's owner to process an exchange of the issue for another. The feature is not reversible.

Convertible Issue. Issue which can be converted (exchanged) to another issue, usually common stock, on demand of the security owner.

Corporate Bond. Long-term debt of a corporation issued with a maturity of 10 to 30 years.

Corporate Notes. Intermediate-term debt of a corporation issued with maturity from 1 to 10 years.

Cost of Carry. Interest expense involved in carrying a position.

Coupon Rate. Rate set to be paid annually by issuer on a debt instrument.

Cumulative Preferred. Dividends not paid and passed over must be paid along with the current dividend before the common stockholder can receive any dividend payment.

Currency Future. A future contract which permits a participant to lock in a rate of exchange of one currency against another.

Current Yield. Return on investment based on current market value. Yield is obtained by dividing current market value into annual interest/dividend payment.

Dealer's Broker. *See* Broker's Broker.

Debenture Bond. Corporate bond backed by nothing but the good name of the issuer.

Delayed Delivery. The settlement date of a transaction is set anywhere between six business days and 60 calendar days after trade date.

Delta. The percentage move of a derivative product to a point move in its underlying issue.

Discounted Instrument. A debt instrument which pays its interest at maturity and is calculated by subtracting the interest amount from face value.

Dollar Price. Market price value display used in some debt instruments. It is actually a percent of the debt's face value.

Dorm. Municipal description for college dormitory issues.

ECU. European currency units. A currency made up of the currencies from nine European countries.

Equipment Trust. Corporate bond secured by the rolling stock of a company such as railroad cars, airplanes, and so on.

European Form of Option. An option which is only exerciseable at the end of its life.

Ex-Distribution Date (Used in Equities). Usually the first business day after payable date. The first day purchasers of an issue will not be entitled to receive some preannounced distribution.

Ex-Dividend Date (Used in Equities). Usually four business days before Record Date. The first day the purchaser of the stock is not entitled to receive the dividend payment.

Expensive. *See* Overvalued.

Falling Out of Bed. Issue, or market, is losing value.

F & A. February and August. Refers to the semiannual months that a particular debt instrument pays interest. *See also* J & J, M & S, A & O, M & N, and J & D.

Far Out Month. Refers to longer or longest duration contract being offered by a derivative product.

Fed Fund Rate. The rate at which banks will lend which they reserve to one another.

Fed Funds. Same day money.

Fill or Kill. Execute the entire order immediately or cancel it.

Firm Quote. The bid or offer at which a transaction can occur as there are interested parties willing to trade at these prices.

Fixed Income Security. An instrument that is to pay a preset amount of income on an annual basis. Corporate bonds are an example.

Fixed Payment Mortgages. *See* FPM.

Flat Position. A position which is neither long nor short.

Floating Rate. Debt involving a rate of interest that is not fixed or pegged to another rate like one weekly treasury auction or LIBOR.

FNMA. Federal National Mortgage Association.

FOK. *See* Fill or Kill.

Forward Contract. Negotiated contract traded over the counter with a delayed delivery.

FPM. Fixed Payment Mortgages. Monthly payment is set over the life of the mortgage.

Freddie Mac. Federal Home Loan Mortgage Corporation.

French Franc. Currency of France.

Future. Sets the price at which a delivery will occur at a later date (some time in the future).

Gamma. The size of a price move as part of volatility.

General Obligation. Debt issued by municipality backed by the full taxing power of the issuer.

GNMA. Government National Mortgage Association.

GO. *See* General Obligation.

Good-til-Canceled. Order that remains in force until it is either executed or canceled.

Got Clock Cleaned. Took a large loss on a situation.

GPM. Graduated Payment Mortgage. A form of mortgage in which the interest rate and therefore the payment gradually increases over the initial years of the mortgage.

Graduated Payment Mortgages. *See* GPM.

GTC. *See* Good-til-Canceled.

Haircut. The percentage of a security's market value subtracted for safety reasons and good conservative accounting procedures. A $100 stock with a 30% haircut is carried on the company's books at a value of $70.

Handle. One hundred points on certain future and option products. Example, an index which moves from 186.8 to 189.8 has moved 3 handles.

Heading South. Product, market, etc., is losing value.

Hedge. Any strategy where potential loss is offset by a contra reacting position. (Example, long U.S. T Bonds, short U.S. T Bonds, futures.)

Holder of Record. Name appearing on a certificate as registered owner to which a dividend or distribution payment will be made. Certificate was registered to that party on record date.

HSD. High school district. Municipal bonds terminology.

IMM. *See* International Monetary Markets.

Immediate or Cancel. An instruction on an order to execute as much as possible immediately and cancel any remaining portion.

Index. A weighted value given to a group of issues.

Interest Rate Swap. Borrower contracts to exchange interest terms on loan for one that fits needs better (i.e., fixed rate or variable).

International Monetary Market (IMM). Offers trading facilities for futures and options on futures products on various currencies and short-term money market instruments. It is part of the Chicago Mercantile Exchange.

In the Money. aka Intrinsic value. A condition existing when the market value of an underlying issue is below the strike price (put) or above the strike price (call) of a given option series.

Intrinsic Value. Refers to a value that must be present in products such as options, warrants, or rights given certain market conditions existing between the surrogate product and base product.

Inverted Yield Curve. A condition that exists when near-term rates are equal or higher than long-term rates.

IOC. *See* Immediate or Cancel.

J & D. June and December. Refers to the semi-annual months that a debt interest pays interest. *See also* J & J, F & A, M & S, A & O, and M & N.

J & J. January and July. Refers to the semi-annual months that a particular debt instrument pays interest. *See also* F & A, M & S, A & O, M & N, and J & D.

KCBT. Kansas City Board of Trade. A futures exchange.

LIBOR. A major source for interest rate setting in the international arena. *See also* London Interbank Offered Rate.

Limited Tax. Type of municipal bond backed by a special tax (i.e., cigarette tax, liquor tax, and so on).

Lira. Currency of Italy.

London Interbank Offered Rate. Rate set against which many loans have the interest cost pegged.

Long Position. A position in which the issue is owned.

LT Tax. *See* Limited Tax.

M & N. May and November. Refers to the semi-annual months that a particular debt instrument pays interest. *See also* J & J, F & A, M & S, A & O, and J & D.

M & S. March and September. Refers to the semi-annual months that the particular debt pays interest. *See also* J & J, F & A, A & O, M & N, and J & D.

Mark to the Market. Process by which securities or positions in an account are adjusted to reflect their current market value.

Market Value. Worth an issue has in the marketplace, and the price at which it can be traded.

Maturity. Point in time when the debt instrument must be paid off by the issuer.

MBIA. Municipal Bond Insurance Association. One of several guarantors of some municipal bonds.

Midwest Stock Exchange. Registered with the SEC and offers trading facilities for equity products.

Minimum Tick. Smallest graduation of trading increment for the particular product.

Modified Pass-Through. A securitized group of mortgages that pay principal and interest on a monthly basis to the security owner.

Moody's. A security rating service.

Mortgage Bond. Corporate debt secured by the value of real estate such as factory or other buildings.

MSE. *See* Midwest Stock Exchange.

Municipal Bond. Intermediate and long-term debt issued by state or local governments.

Municipal Notes. Short-term debt instrument issued by state or local governments.

Municipal Security. Debt issued by state or local governments.

NASD. *See* National Association of Securities Dealers.

National Association of Securities Dealers. Regulator under the SEC of the over-the-counter market.

Near Month. Used in derivative products and refers to the next expiring or maturing month of the product being discussed.

Negative Cost of Carry. When expense in carrying a position exceeds the revenue (interest) received from the instruments.

NH. *See* Not Held.

New York Stock Exchange. Registered exchange with the SEC that offers facilities for the trading of equities, debt and option products. It is a primary self-regulatory organization and a primary equity exchange.

Next Day Settler. Settlement is the business day after trade date.

Not Held. Order executioner not held to time and sales rules of the marketplace. Use professional discretion in executing the order.

NYFE. New York Future Exchange.

NYSE. *See* New York Stock Exchange.

Odd Lot. Quantity smaller than the standard unit of trading. Example, 100 shares is the standard unit of trading (aka, Round Lot). One to ninety-nine shares would be an odd lot.

Offer Price. The part of a quote which represents the lowest price a seller is willing to accept.

Open-end Mortgage Bond. Subsequent issues of the same debt are equal in strength and claim with the open-ended issue.

Open Interest. Number of contracts of options or futures enforced at a point of time.

Option. Gives its owner the privilege of doing something if they desire. If they do not want to, they do not have to, it's their option.

Out of the Money. A condition where the market value of the underlying stock is higher than the strike price (put) or lower than the strike price (call) of a particular option series.

Over-the-Counter Market. The largest of all markets, it operates through a telephone and telecommunication network under the jurisdiction of the NASD.

Overvalued. A perception of a situation which states that the current value or value being applied is overly optimistic or extremely high.

Pacific Stock Exchange. Registered with the SEC, it offers facilities for trading equities and options.

Parity. When the value of two (or more) equivalent products are equal in market value.

Participate But Don't Initiate. An instruction on an order to try and become part of transactions but don't initiate the transaction.

Participating Preferred. A feature found in some preferreds that permit the preferred stockholder to share in extra dividends with the common shareholder, under certain circumstances.

Par Value. Item appearing on a corporate balance sheet that converts shares to dollars (example, 1,000 shares, par value $100 = $100,000). It has nothing to do with book or market value.

Payable Date. The date a dividend, distribution, or interest payment is scheduled to be made.

Peseta. Currency of Spain.

Philadelphia Stock Exchange. Registered exchange with the SEC. The primary exchange for currency options and also offers trading facilities for equity and other option products.

Position Trader. A trader or market maker that maintains positions in the issues being traded versus a trader that buys and sells or sells and buys maintaining a flat position.

Positive Cost of Carry. When the income (interest or dividends) being received on a position exceeds the expense (cost of carry) of maintaining it.

Preferred Stock. Share of ownership in a corporation that is supposed to receive a stipulated rate of dividend. It does not have voting privileges.

PSE. *See* Pacific Stock Exchange.

Put Option. Gives its owner the privilege of selling an underlying issue at a set price for a specific period of time.

Record Date. The date that determines who the legal owners are to receive the payment of dividends, distributions, or interest payments.

Redemption. Process by which certain maturing instruments are retired. The holders of the retiring debt receive cash (principal) in settlement.

Refunding. The retirement of one debt by issuing another.

Regular Way. Settlement cycle of a product (i.e., five business days from trade date to settlement date).

Repo. *See* Repurchase Agreement.

Repurchase Agreement. Financing tool used in U.S. government instrument and certain money market instruments. The instrument is sold with a repurchase agreement in place.

REV. *See* Revenue Bond.

Revenue Bond. Debt instrument issued by Municipality backed by a project from which revenue will be collected (for example, a toll road, bridge fee, etc.).

Reverse Repo. A financing tool. The issue is purchased with the sell back agreement in place. It is the other side of a repo.

Rich. *See* Overvalued.

Rights. Issued under a corporation's charter which contains a preemptive right clause. The existing shareholders are given the right to subscribe to new shares of stock in proportion to their current holdings.

Rollover. A strategy by which the traders trade out of one position into another. It is usually accomplished when one rolls out an expiring or maturing position into the next near-term issue or contract available.

Round Lot. Trading unit of a particular issue, for example, 100 shares of stock, or a $1,000,000 U.S. T Bill is the normal trading unit.

Scalper. A floor trader, usually associated with future trading that trades in and out of positions quickly against the quotes.

SEC. *See* Securities and Exchange Commission.

Securities and Exchange Commission. Federal regulator of the securities industry.

Self-regulatory Organization. An industry agency that has a recognized requirement of policing the industry. The New York Stock Exchange (NYSE) and the National Association of Security Dealer (NASD) are two of these organizations.

Serial Bonds. A bond offering that consists of bonds maturing at different times, found in municipal offerings.

Short Interest. Number of shares of a given issue recorded as being part of short sales as of a specific date. It is reported by the particular marketplace.

Short Position. A security position in which the issue is borrowed and owed to the carrying firm.

Short Sale. Selling an issue not owned or not intended to be delivered. Requires the borrowing of the security.

Sinker. *See* Sinking Fund.

Sinking Fund. A feature found in some corporate bonds that permit the corporation to retire its bond before maturity by acquiring them in the open market and paying for the purchase out of earnings.

Skip Day Settlement. Settlement date is two business days after trade date.

Spot Market. Term used in futures for a future trading in its delivery month.

Spread. Difference between the bid and offer of a quote.

Spread–Option. Simultaneous purchase and sale of equal numbers of put or calls having the same underlying issue and different series.

SRO. *See* Self-Regulatory Organization.

Standard & Poor's. A security rating service.

Standby. A contractual obligation that permits one party to sell mortgage-backed security to another party at a fixed price by a specific date.

Stock dividend. A process by which earnings are distributed by the company buying shares at the stock's par value and distributing them proportionately to the existing shareholders.

Stock Split. Process by which a company can change the market value per share of stock by altering the number of shares outstanding.

Straddle. In the options market, a simultaneous purchase or sale of equal numbers of puts and calls having the same underlying and the same series designation.

Strike Price. Price at which an option contract can be exercised, it is also known as the exercise price.

Subject Quote. Price thought to be current value but must be checked or verified.

Subscription. A process by which existing shareholders have first call on additional shares of that class being issued by the company. *See also* Rights.

Subscription Price. Used in conjunction with a rights offering; amount of dollars needed, along with a finite number of Rights, to purchase newly issued stock.

Swap. A form of trading or strategy where one product or conduction is substituted for another. (Example, a fixed interest rate loan is "swapped" for a variable interest rate loan.)

Swiss Franc. Currency of Switzerland.

Tail. The piece of an instrument which is delivered over and above the contracted amount. It is found in certain instruments such as GNMA. A $1,000,000 trade could be settled with a delivery of $1,002,499.99 issue. The $2,499.99 is the tail.

TBA. *See* To Be Announced.

Time Value. Price paid or received for expectation of value change over the time remaining in the products life.

Times Fixed Charges Earned. Accounting test to determine the corporation's ability to pay its interest expense. It's obtained by dividing earnings by annual interest expense.

To Be Announced. A "when issued" form of trading used in mortgage-backed securities. The pool of mortgages has not been assigned its unique pool number. (The unique pool number is yet to be announced.)

TPKE. Municipal turnpike debt issues.

Trading at a Discount. Market value is below face value or par, or is relatively cheap compared to normal. It is also used when an instrument is selling below intrinsic value.

Trading at a Premium. Market value is higher than face value, or market value is very rich compared to normal, or market value is higher than par.

Trading Flat. Used in debt instruments; the issue being traded does not carry accrued interest.

Undervalued. A perception that stands for the current value or anticipated value of an issue or situation is below what would be fair value.

Unwind. The term used when a trader works out of (close) a position. Many times a strategy involves different positions which must be reduced and offset simultaneously.

U.S. Dollar. Currency of the United States of America.

U.S. T Bills. Short-term debt instrument of the federal government.

U.S. T Bond. Long-term debt of the federal government.

U.S. T Note. Intermediate-term of debt of the federal government.

Volatility. The degree or ability of the market value of an issue, marketplace, index, etc. to change over time.

Warrants. Issued by corporations along with Preferred Stock or Bonds as a unit. It permits the owner to buy an underlying issue from the issuer at a set price for a specific period of time.

Working Capital. Accounting measure, testing the company's ability to pay off current liabilities. It is obtained by dividing current assets by current liabilities.

Workout Quote. Price believed to be possible. The trader needs time to shop the order around.

WW. Waterworks. Municipal debt terminology.

Yen. Currency of Japan.

Yield Curve. A pictorial presentation of yields spread over a time period denoting such data as near-term versus long-term rates.

Yield Equivalent. Comparison of two issues taking into account and adjusting for the idiosyncrasies of one so that it replicates the other.

Yield to Maturity. Rate of return based on annual interest payment plus or minus the difference between the current market value and the value at maturity amortized over the life of the instrument.

Index

A

Accrued interest, 50–51
Active issues, traders of, 52–53
Activity, and profitability, 6
Agency markets, 32
All or none (AON) orders, 27
American Airlines. *See* UAL
    Corporation
American form of option, 176
American Stock Exchange, 38
American Telephone and
    Telegraph, 185, 187
Amortizing, 108
Anticipatory need, 37
Arbitrage trading, 83
Arbitrageurs, 86
At the money options, 162
Auction markets, 32
Average life yields, 73

B

Bankers acceptances (BAs), 3, 73
Basis prices, 102
    and municipal issues, 107–109
Basket trading, 39, 204
Beta, defined, 171, 173
Block trader, 59–60
Block trading, definition, 48
Blue list, 113–118
Bridge Information Systems,
    185–189
Broker call rate, 4

Broker markets, 32
    and dealer market compared,
        32–33
Buy limit orders, 23
Buy market order, 22
Buy stop orders, 23
Buying back issue, 6

C

Calendar spreads, 181
Call, definition, 136
Call feature, 72
Call option, 12, 149
Callable corporate debt, 76–77
Callable debt instruments, 110–112
Callable preferred stock, 97–98
Calls, trading, 134–137. *See also*
    Options traders, calls
Cash flow, 125
Cash settlement products and
    physical settlement products
    compared, 201–203
Certificates of Deposit (CDs), 3, 73
Chartist, 16
Chicago Board of Exchange
    (CBOE), 38
Collateralized Mortgage
    Obligations (CMOs) and
    pass-throughs compared,
    139–142, 144
Combos, 28, 182
Commercial paper (CPs), 3, 73